ALL NEW

100
MATHS
LESSONS

HOMEWORK
& ASSESSMENT

Ann Montague-Smith

YEAR 3

Scottish Primary 4

Credits

Author
Ann Montague-Smith

Editor
Tracy Kewley

Assistant Editor
Margaret Eaton

Illustrations
Garry Davies
Mark Ruffle

Series Designer
Catherine Mason

Designers
Micky Pledge
Melissa Leeke

Text © Ann Montague-Smith © 2006 Scholastic Ltd

Designed using Adobe InDesign

Published by Scholastic Ltd
Villiers House
Clarendon Avenue
Leamington Spa
Warwickshire CV32 5PR

www.scholastic.co.uk

Printed by Bell and Bain Ltd, Glasgow

2 3 4 5 6 7 8 9   6 7 8 9 0 1 2 3 4 5

British Library Cataloguing-in-Publication Data
A catalogue record for this book is available from the British Library.

ISBN 0-439-96515-2
ISBN 978-0439-96515-6

Contents

HOMEWORK

ASSESSMENT

Contents

About the series

All New 100 Maths Homework and Assessment Activities offers a complete solution to your planning and resourcing for maths homework and assessment activities. There are seven books in the series, one for each year group from Reception to Year 6.

Each *All New 100 Maths Homework and Assessment Activities* book contains approximately 60 homework activities, with activity sheets to take home, and assessments for each half term, end of term and end of year.

The homework and assessment activities support planning, based on the National Numeracy Strategy's medium-term plans, but using the language of the learning objectives for that year as they appear in the NNS *Framework for Teaching Mathematics* (DfEE, 1999).

About the homework activities

Each homework activity is presented as a photocopiable page, with supporting notes for parents and helpers provided underneath the activity. Teacher's notes appear in grid format at the beginning of each term's activities. There are unit references in the grids, which link the homework activities to the relevant units in the NNS medium-term plan. There are mostly two homework activities to support each unit. The grids are the only place in the book where the objectives and further detail on the homework are provided. When exactly the homework is set and followed up is left to your professional judgement.

Across the *All New 100 Maths Homework and Assessment Activities* series, the homework activities cover the range of homework types suggested by the National Numeracy Strategy. For Year 3, there are Maths to share activities, Homework activities, Maths homework and Puzzles to do at home.

● **Maths to share activities** encourage the child to discuss the homework task with a parent or carer, and may, for example, involve the home context, or a game to be played with the carer.
● **Homework activities** are timed exercises which encourage the child to work rapidly.
● **Maths homework activities** allow the child to practise skills.
● **Puzzles to do at home** are investigations or problem-solving tasks. Again, the parent or carer is encouraged to be involved with the activity, offering support to the child, and discussing the activity and its outcomes with the child.

Using the homework activities

Each homework page includes a 'Helper note', which explains the aim of the homework and how the adult can support their child if he or she cannot get started. It is recommended that some form of homework diary be used alongside these activities, to promote effective home-school dialogue about the children's enjoyment and understanding of the homework. A homework diary page is provided on page 8 if you do not already have a resource in use. It includes opportunities for a response from the parents and can be sent home with each homework activity.

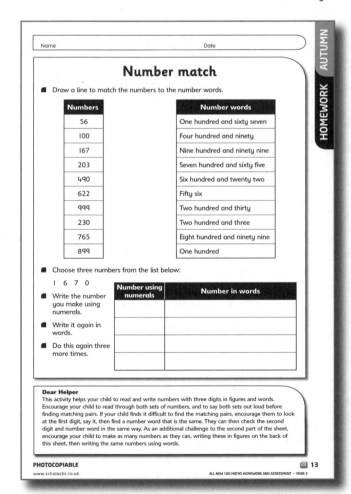

The teacher's notes

The teacher's notes appear at the start of each term's homework activities. They are presented in a grid format. The grid for the homework activities sets out the following:

● The title of the homework.

● Learning objectives: these are linked to the NNS medium-term plan. Where appropriate, the key objective(s) for that unit have a homework activity. This will help as part of on-going teacher assessment to show how well the children have understood the concepts being taught.

● The content of the homework: this shows the type of homework (Maths to share activities, Homework activities, Maths homework and Puzzles to do at home) and briefly describes the format and content of the activity.

● Managing the homework: this section provides 'before' and 'after' information for the teacher. The 'before' notes provide suggestions for ways to introduce and explain the homework before the children take it home. The 'after' notes provide suggestions for how to review the homework when the children return with it to school. Suggestions include marking the work together, discussing strategies used for solving a problem, comparing solutions and playing a game as a class.

● NNS unit reference.

● Page link to *All New 100 Maths Lessons Year 3*. This will enable practitioners who are using this sister book to compare what is being taught that week with the homework, so that the teacher can decide which homework to choose and when to send it home.

Developing a homework policy

The homework activities have been written with the DfES 'Homework guidelines' in mind. These can be located in detail on the Standards Site: **www.standards.dfes.gov.uk/homework/ goodpractice** The guidelines are a good starting point for planning an effective homework policy. Effective home-school partnerships are also vital in ensuring a successful homework policy.

Encouraging home-school links

An effective working partnership with parents and carers makes a positive impact upon children's attainment in mathematics. The homework activities in this book, and the homework diary page on page 8, will support this partnership. Parents and carers are given guidance on what the homework is about, and on how to be involved with the activity. There are suggestions for helping the children who are struggling with a particular concept, such as ways of counting on or back mentally, and extension ideas for children who would benefit from slightly more advanced work. The homework that is set across the curriculum areas for Year 3 should amount to a total of about one and a half hours a week.

The results from the assessment activities can also be used by the teacher in discussions with parents or carers. The outcomes of the activities, which cover the key objectives taught that half-term, term or year, will give good evidence about how well the child is performing for the year group.

NNS OBJECTIVES ▢ Teacher's notes

Activity name	Learning objectives	Content of homework	Managing the homework	All New 100 Maths Lessons Year 3	
				NNS	Page
Number match	● Read and write whole numbers to 1000 in figures and words.	Maths homework Matching numerals and number words for HTU numbers.	**Before:** Explain that the homework will help the children to read and write numbers using figures and words. **After:** Review the homework together. Discuss particularly the numbers 203 and 230, and what the 2, 0 and 3 represent in each of the numbers.	1	8
Partitioning	● Know what each digit represents, and partition three-digit numbers into a multiple of 100, and a multiple of ten, and ones (HTU).	Homework activities Partitioning three-digit numbers into H, T and U.	**Before:** Write 456 onto the board and ask what each digit represents. **After:** Mark the homework together. Check that the children understand what each digit represents. Note how long they took to complete the homework.	1	10
Addition	● Use knowledge that addition can be done in any order to do mental calculations more effectively.	Maths to share Reviewing addition strategies by choosing a strategy to solve each addition question.	**Before:** Explain that you would like the children to identify which of the three strategies they should use to solve each question. Remind them of what the strategies are. **After:** Mark the homework as a class and invite suggestions as to which strategy should be used for each question, and why that is the best one to choose.	2	17
Money puzzle	● Recognise all coins and notes. **Understand and use £.p notation** (for example, know that £3.06 is £3 and 6p).	Puzzles to do at home Finding different totals of three coins.	**Before:** Explain the activity and suggest that some children may find it helpful to use real coins to help them to solve the puzzle. **After:** Review the homework and write the totals onto the board. Ask: *What would be the largest possible total?* (£6) *How did you work that out? What is the smallest possible total?* (60p)	3	21
Telling the time	● Read the time to 5 minutes on an analogue clock and a 12-hour digital clock, and use the notation 9.40.	Maths to share Writing analogue time using digital format and answering some time questions.	**Before:** Remind the children how to count around the clock face in five-minute intervals. **After:** Review the children's answers, particularly those at the bottom of the sheet. Invite the children to work out how long they sleep each night from their answers.	4	28
10 centimetres	● Record estimates and measurements to the nearest whole or half unit (eg 'about 3.5kg').	Maths to share Estimating and measuring lengths of 10cm; devising a way of measuring longer items.	**Before:** Remind the children how to use a ruler, where to place the item against the ruler, and how to read off ½cm. **After:** Review the homework. Discuss how the children used the ruler to measure longer lengths.	4	31

AUTUMN

HOMEWORK

Introduction

Using the activities with *All New 100 Maths Lessons Year 3*

The activities, both homework and assessment, fit the planning within *All New 100 Maths Lessons Year 3*. As teachers plan their work on a week-by-week basis, so the homework activities can be chosen to fit the appropriate unit of work.

For assessment, there are activities to support the 'Assessment lessons' built into the NNS medium-term plan, for example weeks 7 and 14 in the autumn term of Year 3. The assessment tasks are built around the key objectives taught during the preceding half-term and all objectives taught are covered in the appropriate assessment. Further information about using the assessment activities can be found on page 84.

🔲 Homework diary

Name of activity & date sent home	Child's comments		Parent or helper's comments	Teacher's comments
	Did you like this? Draw a face. 🙂 😐 🙁 a lot a little not much	How much did you learn? Draw a face. 🙂 😐 🙁 a lot a little not much		

PHOTOCOPIABLE

NNS OBJECTIVES — Teacher's notes

Activity name	Learning objectives	Content of homework	Managing the homework	All New 100 Maths Lessons Year 3	
				NNS	Page
Number match	● Read and write whole numbers to 1000 in figures and words.	**Maths homework** Matching numerals and number words for HTU numbers.	**Before:** Explain that the homework will help the children to read and write numbers using figures and words. **After:** Review the homework together. Discuss particularly the numbers 203 and 230, and what the 2, 0 and 3 represent in each of the numbers.	1	8
Partitioning	● **Know what each digit represents,** and partition three-digit numbers into a multiple of 100, and a multiple of ten, and ones (HTU).	**Homework activities** Partitioning three-digit numbers into H, T and U.	**Before:** Write 456 onto the board and ask what each digit represents. **After:** Mark the homework together. Check that the children understand what each digit represents. Note how long they took to complete the homework.	1	10
Addition	● Use knowledge that addition can be done in any order to do mental calculations more effectively.	**Maths to share** Reviewing addition strategies by choosing a strategy to solve each addition question.	**Before:** Explain that you would like the children to identify which of the three strategies they should use to solve each question. Remind them of what the strategies are. **After:** Mark the homework as a class and invite suggestions as to which strategy should be used for each question, and why that is the best one to choose.	2	17
Money puzzle	● Recognise all coins and notes. **Understand and use £.p notation** (for example, know that £3.06 is £3 and 6p).	**Puzzles to do at home** Finding different totals of three coins.	**Before:** Explain the activity and suggest that some children may find it helpful to use real coins to help them to solve the puzzle. **After:** Review the homework and write the totals onto the board. Ask: *What would be the largest possible total?* (£6) *How did you work that out? What is the smallest possible total?* (60p)	3	21
Telling the time	● Read the time to 5 minutes on an analogue clock and a 12-hour digital clock, and use the notation 9.40.	**Maths to share** Writing analogue time using digital format and answering some time questions.	**Before:** Remind the children how to count around the clock face in five-minute intervals. **After:** Review the children's answers, particularly those at the bottom of the sheet. Invite the children to work out how long they sleep each night from their answers.	4	28
10 centimetres	● Record estimates and measurements to the nearest whole or half unit (eg 'about 3.5kg').	**Maths to share** Estimating and measuring lengths of 10cm; devising a way of measuring longer items.	**Before:** Remind the children how to use a ruler, where to place the item against the ruler, and how to read off ½cm. **After:** Review the homework. Discuss how the children used the ruler to measure longer lengths.	4	31

NNS OBJECTIVES ▢ Teacher's notes

Activity name	Learning objectives	Content of homework	Managing the homework	All New 100 Maths Lessons Year 3	
				NNS	Page
Sorting 2-D shapes	● Classify and describe 2-D shapes, referring to reflective symmetry, the shape of faces, the number of sides and vertices, whether sides are the same length, whether or not angles are right angles...	**Maths to share** Recognising the properties of 2-D shapes.	**Before:** Check that the children know what a quadrilateral is and can suggest some, such as square and rectangle. **After:** Review the work together. Ask the children to suggest other properties for each of the shapes.	5	34
Holiday map	● Read and begin to write the vocabulary of position, direction and movement: for example, describe and find the position of a square on a grid of squares with the rows and columns labelled.	**Maths to share** Plotting items using coordinates.	**Before:** Check that the children are confident with the convention for writing coordinates. **After:** Review the work together using an A3 enlargement of the sheet. Invite individual children to show where each item belongs.	5	36
Is it true?	● Investigate a general statement about familiar numbers by finding examples that satisfy it.	**Puzzles to do at home** Investigating the properties of squares and rectangles to show that a general statement is true.	**Before:** Remind the children that a statement about shapes can be true or false and that they need to find examples to demonstrate this. **After:** Review the children's findings. Discuss how the properties of rectangles are the same as squares, but that squares have a unique property (all sides equal in length).	6	40
Odd numbers	● Investigate a general statement about familiar shapes by finding examples that satisfy it.	**Puzzles to do at home** Finding examples to match the statement that any odd plus any even number always gives an odd answer.	**Before:** Remind the children that the activity asks them to find examples that match the statement. **After:** Invite children from each ability group to write one of their addition sentences on the board. Discuss how an odd plus an even number always gives an odd answer.	6	42
Odds and evens	● Count on or back in twos, starting from any two-digit number, and recognise odd and even numbers to at least 100.	**Maths homework** Making two-digit numbers and deciding whether each is odd or even.	**Before:** Revise the rule for odd numbers and even numbers. **After:** Invite the children to give some examples of odd and even numbers. Extend this to three-digit examples for the more able.	8	45
Estimating	● Count larger collections by grouping them in tens.	**Maths to share** Estimating quantities and counting them in tens.	**Before:** Practise counting in tens up to about 200 then back again. **After:** Invite the children to discuss how effective they found counting items in tens, and to give reasons for their answers.	8	46

NNS OBJECTIVES 📖 Teacher's notes

Activity name	Learning objectives	Content of homework	Managing the homework	All New 100 Maths Lessons Year 3	
				NNS	Page
Multiplication arrays	● Understand multiplication as repeated addition.	**Maths homework** Drawing multiplication arrays and using equal addition.	**Before:** Remind the children of an array, such as 5 x 3, by asking a child to make it with counters on the OHP. Then ask for the two equal addition sentences that could be made. **After:** Invite children to demonstrate any further multiplications that they generated for themselves with counters and the OHP.	9	52
Times 10 and 100	● To multiply by 10/100, shift the digits one/two places to the left.	**Homework activities** Timed exercise of multiplying single-digit and two-digit numbers by 10 then by 100.	**Before:** Ask: *What happens to the digits when we multiply by 10...100?* **After:** Review the homework together, encouraging the children to say the division sentences, such as 500 ÷ 100 and 500 ÷ 10.	9	54
Find the change	● Solve word problems involving numbers in 'real life', money and measures, using one or more steps, including finding totals and giving change, and working out which coins to pay.	**Puzzles to do at home** Solving money problems of choosing coins and change.	**Before:** Explain the task to the children and tell the less able children that they may use real coins to help them at home. **After:** Ask individual children to explain how they found their results.	10	60
Presents	● **Choose and use appropriate operations (including multiplication and division) to solve word problems,** and appropriate ways of calculating: mental, mental with jottings, pencil and paper, or calculator.	**Maths to share** Problems to solve where children decide which operation to use.	**Before:** Remind the children that they can choose the mathematics to solve a problem. **After:** Discuss which mathematics, and way of calculating, the children chose. Discuss which were the more efficient methods, and why.	10	63
Fraction search	● **Recognise unit fractions 1/2, 1/3, 1/4, 1/5, 1/10 and use them to find fractions of shapes and numbers.**	**Maths homework** Finding the fraction to match the pictures.	**Before:** Recap on unitary fractions, checking that children recognise that, for example, if 4/5 is there, then the separate part is 1/5. **After:** Review the homework together so that the children can mark their own. Invite children to say both fractions for each picture, such as 1/3 and 2/3.	11	70

NNS OBJECTIVES 🗋 Teacher's notes

Activity name	Learning objectives	Content of homework	Managing the homework	All New 100 Maths Lessons Year 3	
				NNS	Page
Fraction shade	● Begin to recognise fractions that are several parts of a whole, such as 2/3 or 3/10.	**Maths homework** Writing the fractions of the shaded part of a shape.	**Before:** Draw a 4 x 2 rectangular array and ask: *How many squares would 3/8 be?* Check for other fractions. **After:** Invite the children to take turns to say the fraction for the shaded part, and the fraction of the unshaded part.	11	73
Find the difference	● Find a small difference by counting up from the smaller to the larger number.	**Homework activities** Timed exercise for finding small differences by counting up.	**Before:** Remind the children of the strategy of counting up from the smaller number to the larger to find small differences. **After:** Mark the work together. Invite children from each ability group to demonstrate how they found the answer.	12	75
My time	● **Use units of time and know the relationship between them (second, minute, hour, day, week, month, year).**	**Maths to share** Answering questions on time to do with the individual child.	**Before:** Read through the activity sheet together. Explain that each question should be answered by the child and that their answers will probably be different from other children's. **After:** Invite the children to feed back their answers, and ask some to write their dates of birth on the board.	12	78
Number sort	● **Solve a given problem by organising and interpreting numerical data in simple lists, tables, and graphs.**	**Puzzles to do at home** Sorting numbers in different ways onto a Carroll diagram.	**Before:** Remind the children of the key features of a Carroll diagram, ie 'Has' and 'Does not have'. **After:** Invite the children to explain one of their sortings. Discuss the range of sortings they could have chosen.	13	84

Name

Date

Number match

■ Draw a line to match the numbers to the number words.

Numbers
56
100
167
203
490
622
999
230
765
899

Number words
One hundred and sixty seven
Four hundred and ninety
Nine hundred and ninety nine
Seven hundred and sixty five
Six hundred and twenty two
Fifty six
Two hundred and thirty
Two hundred and three
Eight hundred and ninety nine
One hundred

■ Choose three numbers from the list below:

1 6 7 0

■ Write the number you make using numerals.

■ Write it again in words.

■ Do this again three more times.

Number using numerals	Number in words

Dear Helper
This activity helps your child to read and write numbers with three digits in figures and words. Encourage your child to read through both sets of numbers, and to say both sets out loud before finding matching pairs. If your child finds it difficult to find the matching pairs, encourage them to look at the first digit, say it, then find a number word that is the same. They can then check the second digit and number word in the same way. As an additional challenge to the second part of the sheet, encourage your child to make as many numbers as they can, writing these in figures on the back of this sheet, then writing the same numbers using words.

Name

Date

Partitioning

- Write these three-digit numbers as hundreds, tens and units. The first one is done for you.

- See how quickly you can do this!

- Draw hands on the first clock face to show when you start.

- Draw hands on the second clock face to show when you finish.

Number	Hundreds	Tens	Units
167	100	60	7
649			
333			
509			
590			
950			
905			
237			

- I took [ ] minutes to do this.

- Write four three-digit numbers of your own.

- Now write them in hundreds, tens and units.

Number	Hundreds	Tens	Units

Dear Helper

This activity helps your child to partition, or separate, three-digit numbers into hundreds, tens and units. If your child is confident with this they should manage the first part of the activity very quickly. If your child is unsure, ask them to write the number again, with the heading H, T and U. Now ask how much each of the digits is worth. For example, in 123, the 1 is worth 100, the 2 is worth 20 and the 3 is worth 3. If your child would like a further challenge, ask them to choose four digits and write as many three-digit numbers as they can, using just these digits.

Name

Date

Addition

◀ Read each of these addition questions carefully.

◀ Decide how you will tackle the problem. You could:

☐ Put the larger number first and count on.

☐ Find near doubles using doubles that you already know.

☐ Bridge through a multiple of 10 then adjust.

◀ Write your answer.

◀ Now put a tick in the column to show which strategy you used.

Question	Answer	Counting on	Using doubles	Bridging
45 + 10				
78 + 6				
34 + 35				
49 + 30				
60 + 28				
84 + 9				
26 + 25				
27 + 70				
41 + 42				
94 + 7				

◀ Explain to someone at home how you worked out the answer to each of these.

Dear Helper
This activity gives your child the opportunity to use addition strategies. For example, putting the larger number first and counting on: 7 + 24 = 24 + 7 = 31; using near doubles: 34 + 35 could be seen, for example, as double 30 add 4 add 5; bridging through multiples of 10: this could be used for 45 + 30, which is 45 + 10 + 10 + 10 = 75. If your child finds any of these strategies difficult to use, or is unsure which strategy to use, then work through the question together, identify the best strategy and write out the steps on paper. If your child enjoys a challenge, then ask them to write their own questions on the back of this sheet, one for each strategy.

Name

Date

Money puzzle

▪ Imagine you have three coins. Each coin is worth more than 10p. You can have more than one of the same coin.

▪ Write ten different totals that you can make with different combinations of coins in the space below.

Dear Helper

This activity helps your child to total money. It is also an investigation. If your child is unsure about how to start, ask: *Which coins could you use?* (20p, 50p, £1 and £2 – the selection could contain a combination of different coins, and some coins could be used more than once in each selection.) Use real coins if this helps and encourage your child to total the coins, starting with the largest coin each time. Challenge your child to order the totals from least to greatest.

Name _____   Date _____

Telling the time

■ Read the times on these clocks.

■ Write the time in digital time. The first one is done for you.

■ Now answer these questions.

1. What time do you get up in the morning? _____

2. What time do you go to bed at night? _____

3. So how long are you out of bed during the day? _____

Dear Helper

This activity helps your child to read and write clock times. The times should be written as digital time. If your child is unsure about this, count together around a clock face, in five-minute intervals, to remind your child where the minute hand points. As a further challenge, ask your child to work out for how long they are asleep in a week... a month... a year!

PHOTOCOPIABLE

www.scholastic.co.uk

10 centimetres

◀ There is a ruler drawn for you on this sheet.

◀ Find things at home which you estimate to be about 10 centimetres long.

◀ Now measure them as accurately as you can to the nearest $\frac{1}{2}$ cm.

◀ Write your estimate and measure in the table.

◀ Do this five more times.

I chose	My estimate	My measure

◀ Now find something that you estimate to be about 20 centimetres in length.

◀ Find a way to measure it using the ruler.

◀ Write what you did here. _____

_____

_____

_____

_____

_____

Dear Helper

This activity helps your child to estimate and measure lengths using centimetres and half centimetres. If your child is unsure about how to use the ruler, show them how to line up the item to be measured with the start of the measuring part of the ruler. To take this further, challenge your child to estimate and measure things that are about 30cm long.

PHOTOCOPIABLE

www.scholastic.co.uk

Sorting 2-D shapes

- ◣ Look carefully at the shapes.

- ◣ Read the shape descriptions.

- ◣ Draw a line from each shape to the correct description.

- ◣ Write the shape's name in the space next to it.

_____

This shape has three sides.
It has a right angle.

_____

This shape is a quadrilateral.
All its sides are the same length.
All its angles are the same size.

_____

This shape has no straight sides.
It is symmetrical.

_____

This shape has all its angles the same size.
It has no right angles.
It has six sides.

_____

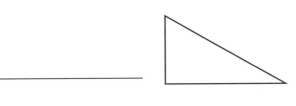

This shape is not a square.
It is a quadrilateral.
It has four right angles.

- ◣ Sketch some quadrilaterals on the back of this sheet.

- ◣ Can you sketch three different ones?

Dear Helper
This activity helps your child to recognise the properties of some 2-D shapes. If your child is unsure about the vocabulary used in the descriptions, read this through together. A quadrilateral is any flat shape with four sides, such as squares and rectangles. To extend the exercise, challenge your child to draw three different pentagons, hexagons and octagons.

Name _____   Date _____

Holiday map

Item	Coordinate
Tents	(b, 2)
Toilet block	(c, 3)
Shop	(d, 4)
Car park	(c, 4)
Play area	(a, 3)
Swimming pool	(d, 5)
Restaurant	(e, 5)

◼ This is a map of a camp site.

◼ Look at where the features on the map belong.

◼ Draw each one in its square.

	a	b	c	d	e
5					
4					
3					
2					
1					

Dear Helper

This activity helps your child to locate positions on a grid. The convention is that the first letter or number represents the columns and the second one the rows. If your child is unsure about this, then plot one of the items together on the map, moving up the column and across the row until the two coordinates meet. Your child may like to add other things to the map and write a list of these and their coordinates.

Name

Date

Is it true?

■ Investigate this sentence:

All squares are rectangles.

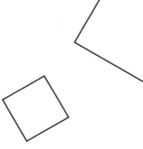

■ Think about the properties of a rectangle.

■ Write them in this box.

■ Now write a sentence to explain if '**All squares are rectangles**' is true.

_____

_____

_____

Dear Helper
This activity helps your child to think about general statements about shape. All squares are rectangles, because rectangles have four right angles, and opposite sides are equal in length. This applies to squares, but squares are special because all of their sides are the same length. If your child is unsure, look at the drawings of the squares, then draw some rectangles and discuss their similarities. You could challenge your child to explain why all squares are quadrilaterals, but all quadrilaterals are not squares.

Name   Date

Odd numbers

◼ Read this sentence:

Any odd number can be made by adding an odd and an even number.

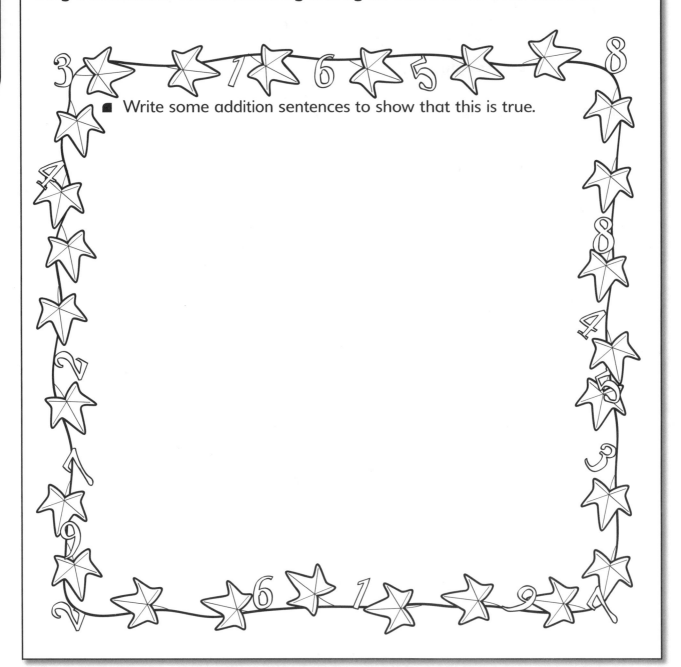

◼ Write some addition sentences to show that this is true.

Dear Helper
This activity helps your child to think about general statements about numbers. If your child is unsure about how to begin, suggest that they choose two small numbers, one odd and one even, then write an addition sentence like this: 5 + 6 = 11, then another one such as 41 + 40 = 81. Ask: *Is the answer odd or even?* Now encourage your child to write some more of these addition sentences to show that the statement is true. Challenge your child to consider whether an odd plus an odd number always gives an even total.

PHOTOCOPIABLE

www.scholastic.co.uk

Name	Date

Odds and evens

◖ Choose two of these numbers each time:

4 5 6 7 8 9

◖ Combine them to make a two-digit number.

◖ Decide whether it is odd or even.

◖ Write it in the table.

Odd	Even

◖ Which is the largest number that you have made? _____

◖ Which is the smallest number that you have made? _____

Dear Helper
This activity helps your child to recognise odd and even two-digit numbers. If your child is unsure whether a number is odd or even, ask them to write a list of odd numbers from 1 to 10, then repeat this for even numbers. This gives the clue: if a number ends in 1, 3, 5, 7 or 9 then it is odd. If it ends in 0, 2, 4, 6 or 8 then it is even. As a further challenge, ask your child to make three-digit numbers and to decide whether each is odd or even.

Name   Date

Estimating

■ Find three large collections of things that you have at home. You might find a tub of marbles, some playing cards and some felt-tipped pens.

■ Write what you have chosen in the table.

    ☐ Look at your first collection. Estimate how many items there are.

    ☐ Write your estimate in the table.

    ☐ Now tip them out and group them in tens.

    ☐ Now count them.

    ☐ Write your results in the table.

■ Do the same for your other collections.

My collection	I estimated	I counted

Dear Helper
This activity helps your child to improve their estimating skills and to count large quantities in tens rather than ones. You may wish your child to put a tray on the table to prevent the items from falling on the floor. If your child is unsure about counting objects in tens, encourage them to group the items into tens. Then, together, count them: 10, 20, 30... Discuss how the ones left over can be counted one by one and added to the count in tens. Challenge your child to think of things in everyday life that could be counted in tens.

Multiplication arrays

■ Read the multiplication sentence.

■ Shade in the multiplication array. The first one is done for you.

■ Write the two equal addition sentences and the answer.

4 x 2 = [ ] [ ] + [ ] = [ ]

[ ] + [ ] + [ ] + [ ] = [ ]

5 x 4 = [ ] + [ ] = [ ]

[ ] + [ ] + [ ] + [ ] + [ ] = [ ]

6 x 3 = [ ] + [ ] = [ ]

[ ] + [ ] + [ ] + [ ] + [ ] + [ ] = [ ]

7 x 3 = [ ] + [ ] = [ ]

[ ] + [ ] + [ ] + [ ] + [ ] + [ ] + [ ] = [ ]

Dear Helper

This activity helps your child to understand that multiplication can be seen as a rectangle of small squares or counters and as equal addition. If your child is unsure, provide some counters, buttons or pennies, and ask them to try setting out a rectangle for 3 x 2. This can be set out as two rows of three or three rows of two. Then ask your child to write the additions: 3 + 3 = 6, and 2 + 2 + 2 = 6. If your child would enjoy a challenge, encourage them to write another five multiplications, drawing the arrays and writing the addition sentences on the back of this sheet.

PHOTOCOPIABLE

www.scholastic.co.uk

Name _____   Date _____

Times 10 and 100

◾ Multiply the first number by 10.

   ☐ Now multiply it by 100.

   ☐ Do the same for the other numbers.

   ☐ See how quickly you can do this!

◾ Draw hands on the first clock face to show when you start.

◾ Draw hands on the second clock face to show when you finish.

Start number	x 10	x 100
5		
8		
4		
9		
7		
1		
10		
30		
80		
90		

Start

Finish

◾ Now write three more of these, choosing your own numbers.

Start number	x 10	x 100

◾ I took [   ] minutes to do this.

Dear Helper

This activity helps your child to understand what happens when we multiply by 10 and by 100. If your child is unsure, write a number such as 2 and say: *What is 2 times 10?* Write the 20 underneath, lining up the 2 of '2' with the '0' of the 20. Now repeat this for multiplying 2 by 100, again lining up the tens and units digits. Encourage your child to explain how the digits shift one place to the left for x 10, and two places for x 100. Challenge your child to divide their answers by 100 and by 10 to check.

www.scholastic.co.uk

Find the change

- Marcus bought a pencil. The pencil cost 16p. He paid for it with one coin.

- Find four different ways to pay.

- Write the change each time as a subtraction sentence.

Marcus chose a [ ] coin.

[ ] p – [ ] p = [ ] p

So his change was [ ] p.

Marcus chose a [ ] coin.

[ ] p – [ ] p = [ ] p

So his change was [ ] p.

Marcus chose a [ ] coin.

[ ] p – [ ] p = [ ] p

So his change was [ ] p.

Marcus chose a [ ] coin.

[ ] p – [ ] p = [ ] p

So his change was [ ] p.

Dear Helper

This activity helps your child to calculate the change due from various coins. If your child is unsure, ask: *Which coin could we use?* Encourage your child to realise that any coin worth less than 20p would not be enough. You may wish to provide some coins to help your child to calculate the change. To extend the activity, challenge your child to provide the change from £2 for other amounts less than £2.

PHOTOCOPIABLE

Presents

- Yasmin wants to buy a present for everyone in her family. She has £10 to spend. She lives with her mother, father and brother Ouni. Ouni is eight years old.

- Help Yasmin decide what to buy.

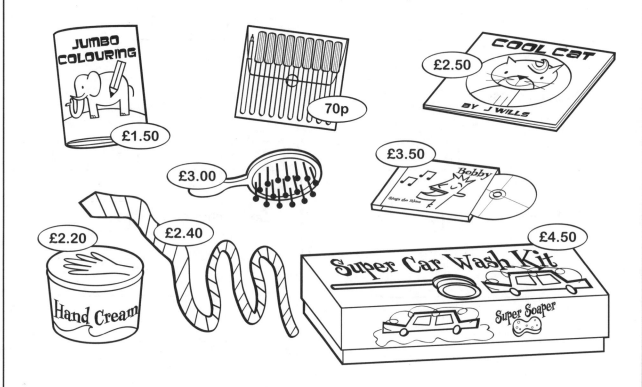

- Yasmin bought her mother a _____ . It cost [ ]

- She bought her father a _____ . It cost [ ]

- She bought her brother a _____ . It cost [ ]

- The presents cost altogether [ ]

- Her change from £10 was [ ]

Dear Helper

This activity helps your child to solve problems, choosing which mathematics to use and how to calculate. Encourage your child to decide which items to buy and to explain how they worked out the total and the change. If your child finds this difficult they will benefit from coins to help them to total the amounts and find the change. Challenge your child to work out how much it would cost if Yasmin had bought everything. Ask: *Would £20 be enough?*

Fraction search

Name
Date

◼ Join each picture to its fraction.

		$\frac{1}{10}$
		$\frac{1}{8}$
		$\frac{1}{4}$
		$\frac{1}{2}$
		$\frac{1}{3}$

Dear Helper
This activity helps your child to recognise the fractions $\frac{1}{2}$, $\frac{1}{3}$, $\frac{1}{4}$, $\frac{1}{8}$, and $\frac{1}{10}$. If your child is unsure, ask: *How many pieces are there altogether? So this one (pointing to the one that is separate) is what fraction?* Challenge your child to say both fractions. For example, the pizza shows $\frac{2}{3}$ and $\frac{1}{3}$.

Name

Date

Fraction shade

◣ Write the fraction for the shaded part of each shape.

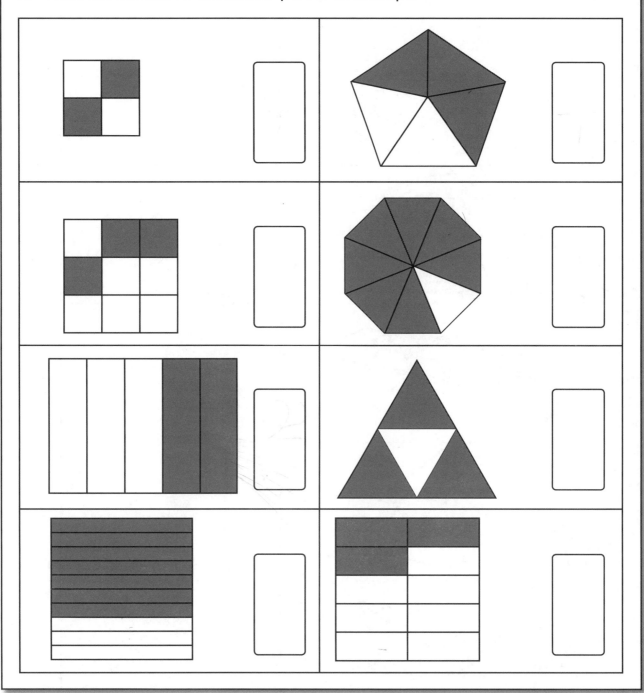

Dear Helper

This activity helps your child to recognise fractions of shapes that are several parts of the whole. If your child is unsure, ask them to count how many parts there are altogether. This will give the denominator (bottom number) of the fraction. Now ask your child to count how many are shaded. This gives the numerator (top number) of the fraction. So, for 8 parts in all and 7 shaded, the fraction is $\frac{7}{8}$. Challenge your child to draw some sets of spots, separate some with a ring, and write the fraction of the separated set.

PHOTOCOPIABLE

www.scholastic.co.uk

Find the difference

- Write the difference between each pair of numbers.

- Remember: you can count up from the smaller number to the larger to do this.

- See how quickly you can do this!

- Draw hands on the first clock face to show when you start.

- Draw hands on the second clock face to show when you finish.

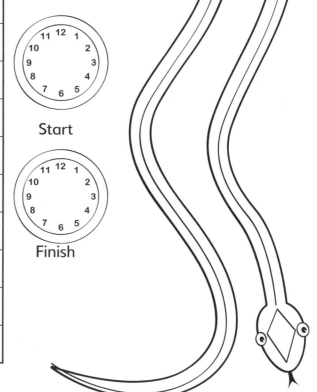

First number	Second number	Difference
16	19	
18	24	
38	42	
87	93	
45	51	
62	57	
52	47	
45	52	
96	87	
98	102	

Start

Finish

- I took [ ] minutes to do this.

Dear Helper
This activity helps your child to practise counting up from the smaller to the larger number in order to find a small difference. If your child finds this difficult, they may find it helpful to use an empty number line. Ask your child to label one end with the lower number, then to decide how many to count on, in ones if necessary, to reach the second number. Now suggest they look for steps on the way. For example, for 34 – 29 they could say *29 and 1 is 30, and 4 more is 34. 1 + 4 is 5, so the difference between 34 and 29 is 5.* You could extend the activity by challenging your child to try some questions such as finding the difference between 197 and 205.

Name _____   Date _____

My time

- ◀ Write the answers to the questions below.

- ◀ Ask for help at home if you are not sure about any answer.

- ◀ You will find the words in the box helpful.

second	minute	hour	day	week	month	year
January	February	March	April	May	June
July	August	September	October	November	December

1. How old are you? _____

2. In which year were you born? _____

3. In which month is your birthday?_____

4. What day is it today? _____

5. What is the date today? _____

6. How many months are there in a year? _____

7. Write something that you think you could do in a minute. _____

_____

8. What is your favourite time of day? _____

_____

9. Why do you like it so much? _____

_____

Dear Helper
This activity encourages your child to read, write and use the vocabulary of time. If your child is unsure how to begin, read the first question together and agree the answer. Continue in this way, reading each question together. If appropriate, challenge your child to work out for how many months they have been born.

PHOTOCOPIABLE

Number sort

- Use the numbers 1 to 20.

- Find a way to sort them onto the Carroll diagram.

- Write headings for the diagram.

- Now write in your numbers.

- Now find another way to sort the numbers 1 to 20 on this Carroll diagram.

Dear Helper

This activity helps your child to sort by one criterion onto a Carroll diagram. When sorting onto a Carroll diagram, one set of numbers has a common property (even numbers, for example); the other set does not have this property and would be labelled 'Not even numbers'. The 'not even' numbers are the odd numbers, but are not labelled like that here. Another way of sorting could be 'Numbers less than 10' and 'Numbers not less than 10'. Discuss different ways of sorting the numbers as there are many ways to do this. Challenge your child to find at least another two ways of sorting the numbers 1 to 20.

NNS OBJECTIVES 🗋 Teacher's notes

Activity name	Learning objectives	Content of homework	Managing the homework	All New 100 Maths Lessons Year3	
				NNS	Page
Number compare	● Compare two given three-digit numbers, say which is more or less, and give a number which lies between them.	**Homework activities** Comparing two three-digit numbers and finding a number to fit between them.	**Before:** Write some pairs of three-digit numbers onto the board and invite suggestions for what could fit between each pair of numbers. **After:** Ask the children to take turns to write one of their pairs of numbers onto the board for others to say what could fit between. Discuss the range of possible answers.	1	90
Race track challenge	● Use knowledge that addition can be done in any order to do mental calculations more efficiently. For example: add three or four small numbers by finding pairs totalling 9, 10 or 11.	**Maths homework** Choosing sets of four small numbers to make totals.	**Before:** Explain that you would like the children to use the strategy of putting the largest number first when tackling this homework. **After:** Review together which numbers the children combined and how they totalled. Discuss which methods were most efficient.	2	96
Add these	● Extend understanding that more than two numbers can be added; add three or four single-digit numbers mentally, or three or four two-digit numbers with the help of apparatus or pencil and paper.	**Maths to share** Deciding whether to use mental methods or pencil and paper to complete some additions.	**Before:** Review the mental strategies that the children have learned for addition. Remind them that sometimes they will find it helpful to use pencil and paper too. **After:** Review the homework together and discuss which strategies were chosen (and why) for each question.	2	97
Sticker problems	● Solve word problems involving numbers in 'real life', money and measures, using one or more steps, including finding totals and giving change, and working out which coins to pay.	**Maths homework** Solving word problems set in a real-life context.	**Before:** Explain to the children that they will need to use their answer to one question to solve the next, and so on. **After:** Review the homework together. Discuss the strategies that the children used to solve the problems.	3	101
Check it	● Check with an equivalent calculation.	**Homework activities** Addition sentences to be checked with an equivalent calculation.	**Before:** Write 20 + 25 on the board and ask how this could be calculated. Ask for suggestions of how to check the answer. **After:** Review the sheet together, discussing in particular the check calculations chosen.	3	105

NNS OBJECTIVES ⬜ Teacher's notes

Activity name	Learning objectives	Content of homework	Managing the homework	All New 100 Maths Lessons Year 3	
				NNS	Page
Find it!	● Make and use right-angled turns and use the four compass points.	**Maths to share** Describing a route using the four compass points.	**Before:** Remind the children of the four points of the compass and how to describe directions. **After:** Review the homework together, and discuss the various solutions that the children have found.	4	110
Making shapes	● Solve mathematical problems or puzzles, recognise simple patterns and relationships, generalise and predict. Suggest extensions by asking *What if...?* **Explain methods and reasoning** orally and, where appropriate, in writing.	**Puzzles to do at home** Investigating which new shapes can be made from cutting an original shape.	**Before:** Discuss the homework task together. Explain that the children should cut off the pieces from the sheet, then sketch each result on another sheet of paper. **After:** Review together the range of shapes that the children found and how they did this. Ask them to suggest extensions to the problem.	4	111
What's the time?	● Read the time to 5 minutes on analogue and 12-hour digital clocks and use the notation 9:40.	**Maths homework** Drawing hands on clock faces to show analogue times for written digital times.	**Before:** Suggest to the children that they may find it helpful to use a clock with hands to ensure that they draw in the hands accurately. **After:** Mark the homework together and discuss any issues that arose for the children whilst doing this homework.	5	113
How heavy?	● Know the relationship between kilograms and grams.	**Maths homework** Reading scales and writing the results for mass.	**Before:** Practise with the children reading some scales for mass. **After:** Invite children from each group to feed back their answers for the others to check their homework.	5	115
What's the problem?	● **Choose and use appropriate operations (including multiplication and division) to solve word problems,** and appropriate ways of calculating: mental, mental with jottings, pencil and paper.	**Maths to share** Calculating answers to number sentences and writing a problem that will fit the number sentence.	**Before:** Discuss the strategies that children could use to solve number problems, including mental strategies, and using paper and pencil to help. **After:** Review the sheet together as the children mark their work. Invite suggestions for the word problems and discuss their suitability.	6	121

NNS OBJECTIVES 🗋 Teacher's notes

Activity name	Learning objectives	Content of homework	Managing the homework	All New 100 Maths Lessons Year 3	
				NNS	Page
Counting patterns	● Describe and extend number sequences: count on in steps of 3, 4 or 5 from any small number to at least 50, and then back again.	**Maths to share** Writing counting sequences in steps of 3, 4 and 5.	**Before:** Count in 3s, 4s and 5s from and back to zero, then from any small number. **After:** Invite the children to suggest their own counting patterns in 3s, 4s and 5s, from and back to any small number.	8	125
Number square challenge	● Investigate a general statement about familiar numbers by finding examples that satisfy it. ● **Explain methods and reasoning** orally and, where appropriate, in writing.	**Puzzles to do at home** Finding squares on the 100-square of four numbers and totalling opposite numbers.	**Before:** Explain the activity to the children, showing them how to identify a square of four numbers on the 100-square. **After:** Review the work together. Ask the children to explain their results.	8	127
Division hops	● **Understand division** as grouping (repeated subtraction) or sharing.	**Maths homework** Dividing by repeated subtraction along a number line.	**Before:** Using a counting stick, ask the children to practise counting back along the stick in 3s, 4s, 5s and 10s. **After:** Review the homework together. Check that the children understand that the jumps on the number line are repeated subtraction.	9	135
Double and halve	● **Recognise that division is the inverse of multiplication,** and that halving is the inverse of doubling.	**Maths to share** Doubling numbers, then halving the result.	**Before:** Practise some doubles, such as double 12, double 14... **After:** Ask the children to explain what happens when a number is doubled then halved.	9	136
Multiplication and division	● Say or write a division statement corresponding to a given multiplication statement.	**Maths to share** Using a known fact to find other facts for multiplication and division.	**Before:** Review some sets of multiplication and division facts, such as 5 x 3 = 15, 3 x 5 = 15, 15 ÷ 3 = 5 and 15 ÷ 5 = 3. **After:** Mark the homework together and discuss how a known multiplication or division fact helps us to find three other facts.	10	138

Activity name	Learning objectives	Content of homework	Managing the homework	All New 100 Maths Lessons Year 3	
				NNS	Page
Calculation check	● Check subtraction with addition, halving with doubling and division with multiplication.	**Homework activities** Solving a number sentence and writing a check calculation.	**Before:** Explain to the children that for each number sentence they are expected to write a check calculation. **After:** Review the homework, paying particular attention to the check calculations. Discuss whether these were sensible ones, and why the children think that.	10	141
Fraction shade	● Begin to recognise simple equivalent fractions, e.g. five tenths and one half, five fifths and one whole.	**Maths homework** Shading equivalent fractions.	**Before:** Explain that the children are to write two fractions, such as 1/2 and 2/4, that are equivalent to the shaded part of each shape. **After:** Invite the children to discuss which fractions they shaded. Discuss the range of possible answers.	11	146
Fraction match	● Begin to recognise simple equivalent fractions, e.g. five tenths and one half, five fifths and one whole.	**Maths to share** Fraction pelmanism game.	**Before:** Remind the children of some equivalent fractions. Write up 1/2 and ask for suggestions of equivalent fractions. **After:** The children can play the game in pairs for a few minutes as a starter activity.	11	149
Venn diagram sort	● **Solve a given problem by organising and interpreting numerical data in simple lists, tables, and graphs,** for example Venn diagrams (one criterion).	**Maths homework** Sorting data onto a one-region Venn diagram.	**Before:** Discuss with the children how to fill in a Venn diagram. **After:** Mark the homework together. Discuss which numbers belong inside the circle and which outside, and why.	12	153

Name   Date

Number compare

- Read each pair of numbers.

- Write any number that fits between them.

- See how quickly you can do this!

142		378
321		954
322		721
549		553
647		892
206		360

- Draw hands on the first clock face to show when you start.

- Draw hands on the second clock face to show when you finish.

- I took [   ] minutes to do this.

- Now write your own pairs of numbers with a number that fits between.

Start

Finish

Dear Helper

This activity helps your child to compare two numbers and to recognise which numbers fit between them. If your child is unsure, begin with a pair of two-digit numbers, such as 25 and 30. Ask: *Which is the larger number? Which is the smaller number? Which numbers go between 25 and 30?* Repeat this for the pairs of three-digit numbers on this sheet. Challenge your child to write some pairs of four-digit numbers and a number that will go between each pair.

Name   Date

Race track challenge

◼ Each car on the race track has a number.

◼ Choose four of the car numbers.

◼ Write the numbers in the order in which you will total them. Remember to put the largest number first.

◼ Write the totals.

Dear Helper
This activity encourages your child to add several small numbers, beginning with the largest number. Once your child has chosen their set of numbers, discuss where they will start, and in which order they will total the other numbers. If they find this difficult, remind them of other strategies to try. For example, for 14 + 5 + 4 + 6 they could look for a pair that makes 10 (4 + 6) so 14 + 10 + 5 = 24 + 5 = 29. To take it further, challenge your child to try totalling more than four small numbers.

www.scholastic.co.uk   ALL NEW 100 MATHS HOMEWORK AND ASSESSMENT · YEAR 3

Name   Date

Add these

- Write the answers to these addition sentences.

- Decide whether to use mental methods or a paper-and-pencil method such as an empty number line.

- Tick the box for the strategy that you used.

Question	Answer	Tick the strategy you used	
		Mental methods	Paper and pencil
9 + 5 + 6 + 4			
6 + 8 + 4 + 7			
5 + 9 + 8 + 4			
17 + 4 + 8 + 3			
15 + 8 + 5 + 9			
13 + 5 + 7 + 8			
12 + 14 + 6 + 5			
19 + 13 + 7 + 2			
16 + 5 + 12 + 8			
19 + 7 + 4 + 6			

- Now find three different ways to make a total of 30. Use four numbers each time.

☐ + ☐ + ☐ + ☐ = ☐

☐ + ☐ + ☐ + ☐ = ☐

☐ + ☐ + ☐ + ☐ = ☐

Dear Helper

This activity helps your child to use mental strategies such as putting the larger number first, finding two numbers that make a 10, adding numbers such as 9, 11 and 19 by adding a 10 or 20 and adjusting by 1. If your child is unsure about the mental strategies, they may find it helpful to use a paper-and-pencil method, such as partitioning the numbers, for example 8 + 9 + 7 = 9 + 1 + 7 + 7 = 10 + 14 = 24. Alternatively, they may find it helpful to use the empty number line. Encourage your child to explain which method they would prefer to use for each question. If they still find this difficult, discuss which method might be good to try, and talk this through together. As an additional challenge, encourage your child to write four further number sentences, this time for a total of 50.

PHOTOCOPIABLE

Sticker problems

- Jamie likes to collect football stickers. Here are some problems about Jamie and his stickers.

- You will need to use the answer to the first problem to solve the next one, and so on.

- There is space for you to make jottings.

---

1. Jamie used his pocket money to buy some stickers. He bought 15 English football stickers, double that number of Scottish stickers, and 20 Welsh ones.

How many did he buy altogether?

[ ]

---

2. When Jamie got to school the next day he decided to give his best friend, Jon, half of his Scottish stickers.

How many stickers did he have left in total? [ ]

---

3. On the way home from school Jamie decided to call in to see his cousin, Ellie. Ellie also likes to collect stickers and she has a total of 47 stickers. They looked at their stickers together. Jamie gave Ellie 10 of his stickers.

How many stickers does Jamie have now? [ ]

How many stickers does Ellie have now? [ ]

---

4. Jamie's dad gave Jamie another 30 stickers. However, Jamie already had 13 of these so he decided to give the 13 to his friend Jon.

How many stickers does Jamie have now? [ ]

Dear Helper

This activity contains lots of detail in each of the problems. If your child is unsure, talk through the problem and agree which information is essential, and which can be ignored. Now work through the problem together, deciding which mathematics is needed to solve it. Challenge your child to invent a new problem about Jamie and his stickers.

Check it

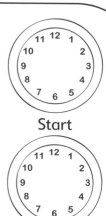

Start

Finish

■ Write your answers to the number statements in the box.

☐ Write your check calculation in the checking box.

☐ See how quickly you can do this!

■ Draw hands on the first clock face to show when you start.

■ Draw hands on the second clock face to show when you finish.

Number sentence	Answer	Check calculation
40 + 24		
36 + 40		
11 + 7 + 19		
16 + 5 + 8		
19 + 8 + 3		
50 + 37		
20 + 77		
12 + 18 + 6		
31 + 10 + 8		
47 + 40		

Dear Helper

This activity helps your child to find a way of checking calculations. Your child could, for example, add in a different order; they could partition the numbers, so for 20 + 25: 20 + 20 + 5 = 40 + 5 = 45; or they could try a subtraction, so for 20 + 25 they could try 45 – 20. If your child is unsure, discuss which strategy they might like to try. Your child can use an empty number line if they find this helpful. Challenge your child to complete the work as quickly and accurately as they can.

PHOTOCOPIABLE

www.scholastic.co.uk

Find it!

- Here is a plan of the park. Each little square is one step.

- Decide which way to go: north, south, east or west.

- Decide how many steps forward to take as you start off.

- Remember you can make right-angled turns.

- Write the directions from the gate to the bench.

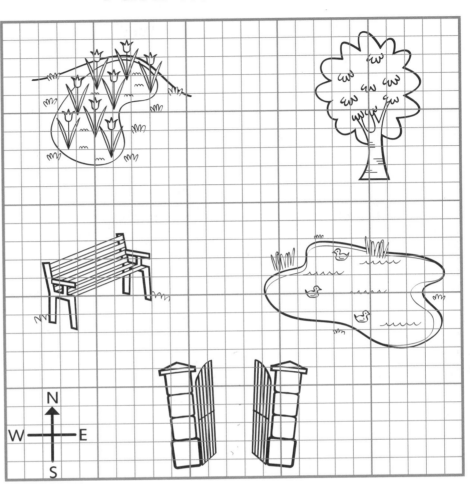

_____

- Write directions from the bench to the tree.

_____

_____

- Now draw in a statue. Write directions from your statue to the gate.

_____

_____

Dear Helper

This activity helps your child to recognise the points of the compass and encourages them to use right-angled turns when giving directions. If your child is unsure, trace the route from the gate to the bench with a pencil. Now discuss whether the movement is north, south, east or west. Count the number of moves forward. Discuss if a right-angled turn is needed. You could challenge your child to write directions for visiting everything in the park once, starting from the gate.

PHOTOCOPIABLE

Name _____ Date _____

Making shapes

■ You will need a pair of scissors, a pencil and another sheet of paper.

■ On this sheet there are several L shapes. Cut these out carefully.

■ Now take one of your shapes.

  □ Cut one of the squares and remove a right-angled triangle.

  □ Make as many different shapes as you can by cutting off one right-angled triangle. You can only make **one** straight cut each time.

  □ Check each time that you have made a new shape by turning it and flipping it.

  □ Sketch each shape that you make on another sheet.

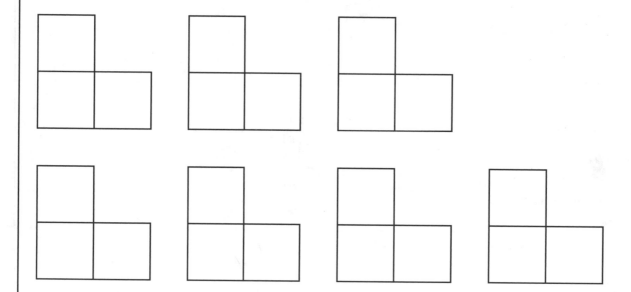

■ How many different shapes did you find? _____

■ Now try again.

  □ Cut off **two** right angled-triangles each time.

  □ How many different shapes can you make now? _____

Dear Helper
This activity helps your child to investigate shape problems. Discuss how they will begin and encourage them to turn and flip each shape they make to check that it is a new shape. Your child may find it helpful to use a mirror to see what the reflection will be. There are three different shapes that can be made. The second part of the sheet is a challenge and there are up to six different shapes that can be made.

Name   Date

What's the time?

◼ Read the time next to each clock.

◼ Draw in the hands to show that time.

 | `3.00` |  | `6.30`

 | `9.45` |  | `4.15`

 | `10.05` |  | `8.20`

 | `7.50` |  | `5.25`

 | `1.35` | | `11.40`

Dear Helper

This activity helps your child to relate digital and analogue time. If your child finds it difficult to draw in the hands accurately, provide a clock with hands and ask them to set the time on it to match the digital time. Ask your child to describe where the hands are, then to draw the hands on the clock on this sheet. Challenge your child to be the timekeeper for a day, saying what the time is at regular intervals throughout the day.

PHOTOCOPIABLE

Name

Date

How heavy?

■ Look carefully at each of these scales.

■ Write how much the item on the scales weighs.

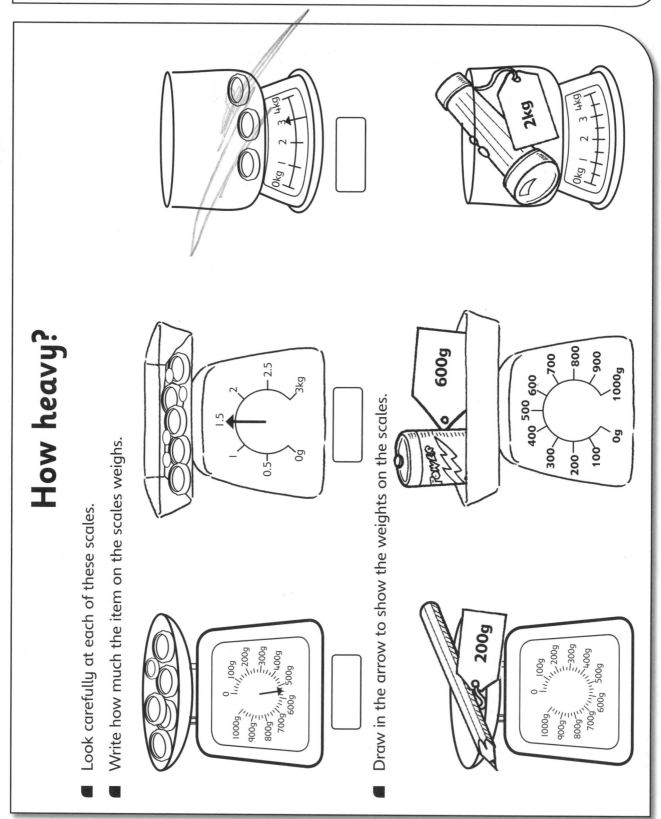

■ Draw in the arrow to show the weights on the scales.

Dear Helper

This activity helps your child to read from scales and to mark a scale reading accurately. If your child is unsure, ask them to count along the markings on the scale to say what each one represents. For a reading of 400g this will be straightforward, but for 550g your child will need to recognise that this is halfway between the 500g and 600g marks. Challenge your child to suggest where readings such as 750g would come on the scale to 3kg.

PHOTOCOPIABLE

www.scholastic.co.uk

Name

Date

What's the problem?

- Write the answer to each number sentence.
- Now write a word problem to match the number sentence.

Number sentence	Answer	Word problem
36 + 15		
42 ÷ 5		
91 – 87		
☐ × 4 = 36	36	

Dear Helper
This activity helps your child to make decisions about which mathematics to use, and whether to use mental strategies or to make jottings as well. It also helps them to think about word problems involving numbers. If your child is unsure how to begin, discuss which mathematics will be needed and how this can be worked out. Then ask your child to put the numbers into a sentence to make a word problem. Challenge your child to write problems that also contain information that is not needed to help solve them.

Name

Date

Counting patterns

◼ Write a number pattern for counting in 3s.

☐ Decide which number from 0 to 2 you will start on.

☐ Continue the pattern until the boxes are all full.

◼ Now write a counting pattern for counting in 4s.

☐ Decide which number from 0 to 3 you will start on.

☐ Continue the pattern until the boxes are all full.

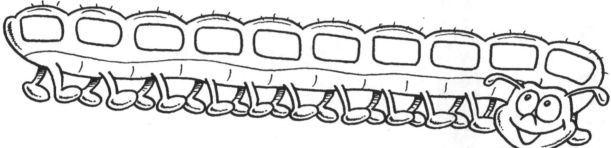

◼ Write a counting pattern for counting in 5s.

☐ Decide which number from 0 to 4 you will start on.

☐ Continue the pattern until the boxes are all full.

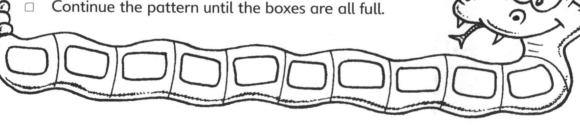

Dear Helper
This activity helps your child to count on from a small number in 3s, 4s and 5s. If your child is unsure, ask them to write out the numbers from 0 to 30. Now say: *Which number shall we start on for counting in 3s?* Then circle each number that comes in the pattern. Challenge your child to write patterns for counting in 6s, starting on any number from 0 to 5.

Name   Date

Number square challenge

- Look at the number grid. The four numbers 1, 2, 11 and 12 make a small number square.

- Add opposite numbers like this:

  1 + 12 = 13

  2 + 11 = 13

1	2	3	4	5	6	7	8	9	10
11	12	13	14	15	16	17	18	19	20
21	22	23	24	25	26	27	28	29	30
31	32	33	34	35	36	37	38	39	40
41	42	43	44	45	46	47	48	49	50

- Now choose your own four numbers that make a small square.

  ☐ Draw a square around your numbers on the number grid.

  ☐ Add opposite numbers.

  ☐ Do this three more times.

I chose [ ] [ ] [ ] [ ]   I chose [ ] [ ] [ ] [ ]

[ ] + [ ] = [ ]   [ ] + [ ] = [ ]

[ ] + [ ] = [ ]   [ ] + [ ] = [ ]

I chose [ ] [ ] [ ] [ ]   I chose [ ] [ ] [ ] [ ]

[ ] + [ ] = [ ]   [ ] + [ ] = [ ]

[ ] + [ ] = [ ]   [ ] + [ ] = [ ]

- What do you notice about your results?

  ☐ Write some sentences to explain your results on the back of this sheet.

Dear Helper

This activity encourages your child to think about why opposite numbers in a number square make equal totals. If your child finds this difficult, break each number down into tens and units. So, for the square 1, 2, 11 and 12, the opposite numbers 1 and 12 contain 1 + 10 + 2, and the opposite numbers 2 and 11 contain 2 + 10 + 1. Each total contains the same digits, but not in the same order. Challenge your child to choose larger squares, such as a 3 × 3 square, total opposite corner numbers and explain their results.

Name _____ Date _____

Division hops

■ Use the number line to help you to solve these division questions.

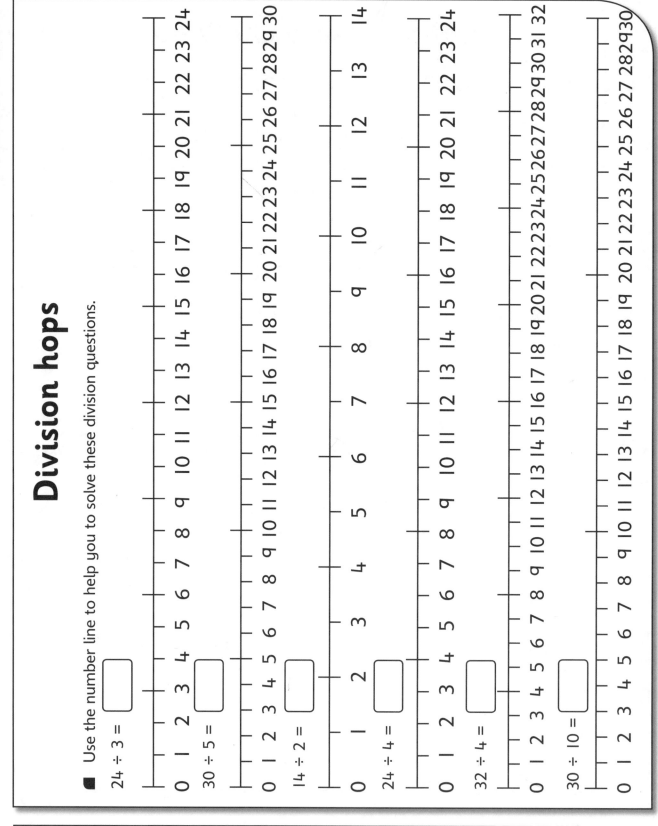

$24 \div 3 =$ ☐

0 1 2 3 4 5 6 7 8 9 10 11 12 13 14 15 16 17 18 19 20 21 22 23 24

$30 \div 5 =$ ☐

0 1 2 3 4 5 6 7 8 9 10 11 12 13 14 15 16 17 18 19 20 21 22 23 24 25 26 27 28 29 30

$14 \div 2 =$ ☐

0 1 2 3 4 5 6 7 8 9 10 11 12 13 14

$24 \div 4 =$ ☐

0 1 2 3 4 5 6 7 8 9 10 11 12 13 14 15 16 17 18 19 20 21 22 23 24

$32 \div 4 =$ ☐

0 1 2 3 4 5 6 7 8 9 10 11 12 13 14 15 16 17 18 19 20 21 22 23 24 25 26 27 28 29 30 31 32

$30 \div 10 =$ ☐

0 1 2 3 4 5 6 7 8 9 10 11 12 13 14 15 16 17 18 19 20 21 22 23 24 25 26 27 28 29 30

Dear Helper

This activity helps your child to recognise that division can be seen as repeated subtraction. If your child is unsure about how to begin the activity, they can count along the number line in hops. So, for 24 ÷ 3, they count how many 3s there are from 0 to 24. Or, they can count back along the line. If appropriate, challenge your child to try some more difficult division questions, such as 48 ÷ 6; 56 ÷ 8.

www.scholastic.co.uk

Name

Date

Double and halve

◢ Write the double of each number in the first box.

◢ Now write half of that number in the second box.

◢ The first one is done for you.

20 ⟶ | 40 | ⟶ | 20 |

15 ⟶ [ ] ⟶ [ ]

14 ⟶ [ ] ⟶ [ ]

9 ⟶ [ ] ⟶ [ ]

18 ⟶ [ ] ⟶ [ ]

16 ⟶ [ ] ⟶ [ ]

◢ Now try these.

12 x 2 = [ ]   24 ÷ 2 = [ ]

13 x 2 = [ ]   26 ÷ 2 = [ ]

17 x 2 = [ ]   34 ÷ 2 = [ ]

19 x 2 = [ ]   38 ÷ 2 = [ ]

◢ Write two of these for yourself.

[ ] x 2 = [ ]   [ ] ÷ 2 = [ ]

[ ] x 2 = [ ]   [ ] ÷ 2 = [ ]

Dear Helper

This activity helps your child to make the link between doubling and halving, and to recognise that division is the inverse, or opposite, of multiplication. If your child finds this difficult, double the tens digit, then the units digit and add the results in order to find the double. For halving, ask: *What do we double to make 34? Yes, 17. So half of 34 is 17.* Challenge your child to write some more difficult number sentences like these.

Name   Date

Multiplication and division

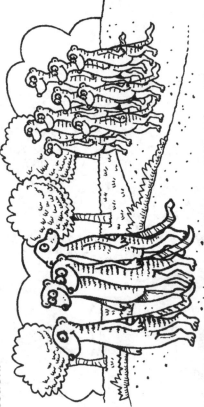

- Write the answer to the first multiplication question.

☐ Use the same numbers to write another multiplication sentence.

☐ Now use the same numbers to write two division sentences.

☐ Fill in the rest of the table, using the numbers that are given to you.

- The last set has been done for you.

Multiplication	Multiplication	Division	Division
5 x 4 =			
6 x 3 =			
		24 ÷ 3 =	
		30 ÷ 5 =	
9 x 10 =			
9 x 4 = 36	4 x 9 = 36	36 ÷ 4 = 9	36 ÷ 9 = 4

Dear Helper

This activity helps your child to recognise that if they know one multiplication or division fact then they can work out three other facts. If your child is unsure about how to begin, discuss which multiplication table the numbers belong to. Encourage your child to say the multiplication table to find the fact. Extend this activity by challenging your child to write some more linked facts like these.

PHOTOCOPIABLE

www.scholastic.co.uk

Calculation check

- Write the answer to the number sentence.
- Write a check calculation to show that you have the correct answer. Remember you can check:

  □ subtraction with addition   □ addition with subtraction   □ halving with doubling
  □ multiplication with division   □ division with multiplication

- See how quickly you can do this. Time how long it takes.

Number sentence	Jottings	Check calculation
26 + 45 =		
42 ÷ 6 =		
92 – 87 =		
16 x 2 =		
Half of 38 =		

- I took [ ] minutes to do this.

Dear Helper

This activity helps your child to recognise which type of check calculation is appropriate for each operation. If your child is unsure, ask them to explain how they solved the number sentence. Then ask them to think of which operation (+ , –, x or ÷) they could use to take them back to the start number. Challenge your child to find different ways of checking, such as adding in a different order.

Fraction shade

- Look carefully at the first shape.
- Decide what fraction has been shaded.
- Now write two fractions that would fit this.
- The first one has been done for you.

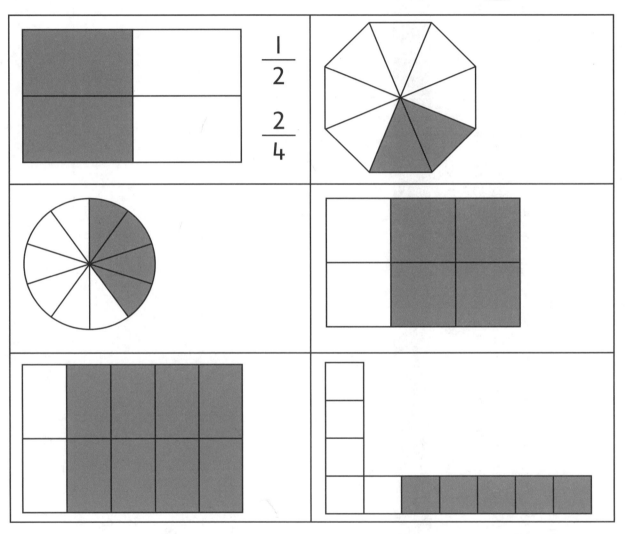

$\frac{1}{2}$

$\frac{2}{4}$

Dear Helper

This activity helps your child to recognise and record two fractions that are equivalent, or worth the same, such as $\frac{1}{2}$ and $\frac{2}{4}$. If your child is unsure about this, encourage them to count how many parts there are in total to the shape and write this as the bottom number of the fraction. Now ask them to count how many parts have been shaded and write this as the top number of the fraction. This gives them a fraction. Discuss how else this could be written, for example $\frac{6}{10}$ is also $\frac{3}{5}$. You could challenge your child to draw some more shapes, shade equal parts and write two fractions for each. They can do this on the back of this sheet.

www.scholastic.co.uk

Name _____   Date _____

$\dfrac{3}{6}$	$\dfrac{4}{8}$	$\dfrac{2}{4}$	$\dfrac{1}{2}$
$\dfrac{6}{8}$	$\dfrac{3}{4}$	$\dfrac{2}{8}$	$\dfrac{1}{4}$
$\dfrac{4}{6}$	$\dfrac{2}{3}$	$\dfrac{2}{6}$	$\dfrac{1}{3}$
$\dfrac{6}{10}$	$\dfrac{3}{5}$	$\dfrac{2}{10}$	$\dfrac{1}{5}$

Fraction match

■ You can play this game with a partner.

☐ Cut out the fraction cards and shuffle them.

☐ Place the cards face down on the table in front of you.

☐ Now turn over two cards.

☐ If the fractions are worth the same, keep the cards.

☐ If the cards do not match, then turn them back down again.

☐ Try to remember where each fraction is!

■ The winner is the player with the most cards at the end of the game.

Dear Helper

Play this game together. The idea is to make pairs of equivalent fractions, such as $\frac{1}{2}$ and $\frac{2}{4}$; $\frac{1}{3}$ and $\frac{2}{6}$; and so on. If your child is unsure about this, then suggest that they draw the fraction. So, for $\frac{2}{6}$ they could draw a rectangle split into six equal strips and shade in two of these. Discuss how this is the same as $\frac{1}{3}$. Challenge your child to play 'Snap' with you with the cards, playing as quickly as you both can.

Name _____   Date _____

Venn diagram sort

◢ Use the numbers from 20 to 50.

◢ Sort them onto the Venn diagram.

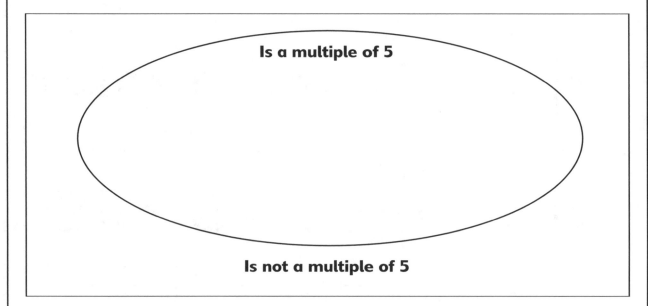

Is a multiple of 5

Is not a multiple of 5

◢ Now sort the numbers from 20 to 50 onto this Venn diagram.

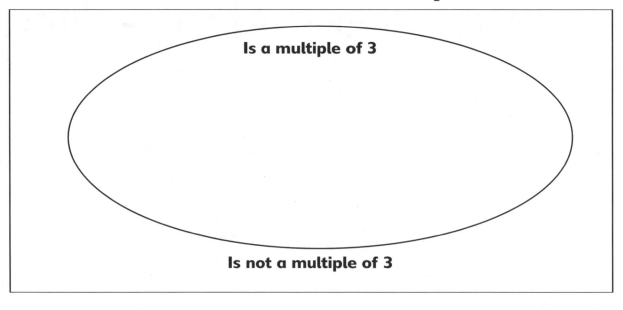

Is a multiple of 3

Is not a multiple of 3

Dear Helper

This activity helps your child to sort data onto a Venn diagram. Inside the circle your child should put the 'multiple of 5' numbers. Outside the circle, but inside the rectangle, is where all the other numbers go. If your child is unsure, suggest that they write out all the numbers from 20 to 50. Now ask them to circle each number that comes in the count of 5s. Discuss where these numbers fit, and where the other numbers go. Repeat this for multiples of 3. Challenge your child to repeat this, this time for multiples of 4.

NNS OBJECTIVES 🗋 Teacher's notes

Activity name	Learning objectives	Content of homework	Managing the homework	All New 100 Maths Lessons Year 3	
				NNS	Page
Number order	● Order whole numbers to at least 1000, and position them on a number line.	**Homework activities** Ordering given numbers onto a number line.	**Before:** Draw an empty number line on the board and write some three-digit numbers. Ask the children to order these onto the line. **After:** Review the homework together, discussing any issues that arise.	1	162
Adding and adjusting	● Add and subtract mentally a 'near multiple of 10' to or from a two-digit number by adding or subtracting 10, 20, 30... and adjusting.	**Maths homework** Choosing two-digit numbers to add to near multiples of 10.	**Before:** Read through the homework instructions with the children and check that they understand what they have to do. **After:** Ask for answers from the children. If anyone has invented their own puzzle, invite them to set it for others to try.	2	170
Number patterns	● Use patterns of similar calculations.	**Maths to share** Continuing addition and subtraction number patterns.	**Before:** Write up 54 – 5, then 54 –15, and so on. Ask the children to say the answers and what comes next. **After:** Mark the homework together. Check that the children have understood the patterns and can continue them.	2	171
Add and subtract	● Use informal pencil-and-paper methods to support, record or explain addition and subtraction of hundreds, tens and units.	**Maths to share** Using empty number lines to add and subtract.	**Before:** Write up some examples of addition and subtraction using an empty number line and work through these together. **After:** Mark the homework together and discuss any difficulties or issues about it that the children found.	3	174
How much? (1)	● Solve word problems involving numbers in 'real life', money and measures, using one or more steps. ● **Check with an equivalent calculation.**	**Maths homework** Solving word problems.	**Before:** Discuss how to check an answer by using an equivalent calculation. **After:** Review the homework together, and invite children from each ability group to explain which check calculation they carried out, and why.	3	176
Measuring bonanza	● Suggest suitable units and measuring equipment to estimate or measure capacity.	**Maths to share** Choosing suitable units for measuring capacities.	**Before:** Review the relationship between millilitres and litres. **After:** Discuss the children's choices for units and containers.	4	181
How much? (2)	● Read scales to nearest division (labelled or unlabelled).	**Maths homework** Reading scales for litres and millilitres.	**Before:** Put some liquid into containers with scales and invite the children to read off how much is there. **After:** Mark the homework together and discuss any difficulties that the children found.	4	183

NNS OBJECTIVES ▢ Teacher's notes

Activity name	Learning objectives	Content of homework	Managing the homework	All New 100 Maths Lessons Year 3	
				NNS	Page
Measures word problems	● **Choose and use appropriate operations (including multiplication and division) to solve word problems,** and appropriate ways of calculating: mental, mental with jottings, pencil and paper.	**Maths homework** Solving word problems set in the context of measures, deciding which way to calculate.	**Before:** Remind the children that they can use mental, mental with jottings, and pencil-and-paper methods to solve these problems. **After:** For each problem, discuss the chosen methods and why these were chosen to solve the problem.	5	184
Is it symmetrical?	● **Identify and sketch lines of symmetry in simple shapes, and recognise shapes with no lines of symmetry.**	**Maths to share** Identifying lines of symmetry, and shapes with no symmetry.	**Before:** Remind the children that not all shapes have lines of symmetry, and that some shapes have more than one line of symmetry. **After:** Mark the homework together, checking that the children are clear about where the lines of symmetry are.	5	187
What's my shape?	● Investigate general statements about shapes by finding examples that satisfy it. ● **Explain methods and reasoning** orally and, where appropriate, in writing.	**Puzzles to do at home** Finding shapes to satisfy a general statement.	**Before:** Say: *I am thinking of a 2-D shape with no straight sides. What could my shape be?* Discuss the possibilities. **After:** Review the homework together. Discuss the children's findings and how they worked out the answers.	6	192
Multiples of 2, 5 and 10	● Recognise two-digit and three-digit multiples of 2, 5 and 10.	**Homework activities** Circling and providing examples of multiples.	**Before:** Ask: *How can we recognise a multiple of 2... 5... 10?* **After:** Mark the homework together, checking that the children have understood how to recognise these multiples.	8	193
Multiples of 50 and 100	● Recognise three-digit multiples of 50 and 100.	**Maths homework** Sorting three-digit numbers to find multiples of 50 and of 100.	**Before:** Count in 50s from 0 to 1000 and back again. Repeat for counting in hundreds. **After:** Say some three-digit numbers. Ask the children to put their hands up if it is a multiple of 50 and to stand if it is a multiple of 100. They stay in their seats if it is neither.	8	194
Remainder search	● Begin to find remainders after simple division.	**Maths to share** Finding which divisors into 24 leave remainders.	**Before:** Ask division questions which have remainders, such as 25 ÷ 4. **After:** Review the children's findings. Check that they have found which divisors into 24 leave a remainder and what that remainder is.	9	198

Activity name	Learning objectives	Content of homework	Managing the homework	All New 100 Maths Lessons Year 3	
				NNS	Page
Division problems	● Begin to find remainders after simple division. ● Round up or down after division, depending on the context. ● Solve word problems involving numbers in 'real life', using one or more steps.	**Maths homework** Solving division problems and deciding whether to round up or down to find the solution.	**Before:** Say: *There are 35 children in the class. Everyone would like a biscuit. If biscuits come in packs of ten, how many packs do I need?* Discuss how the answer will round up to 4. **After:** Review the homework, discussing for each question whether the answer rounds up or down.	9	200
Multiplying and dividing by 10 and 100	● Use known number facts and place value to carry out mentally simple multiplications and divisions.	**Homework activities** Quickly writing the answers to multiplication and division by 10 and 100.	**Before:** Ask: *What happens when we multiply by 10... 100?* **After:** Mark the homework together and check that the children understand what happens to the digits when they are multiplied by 10 or 100.	10	204
Tens and units multiplication	● Use known number facts and place value to carry out mentally simple multiplications and divisions.	**Maths homework** Multiplying the tens, then the digits and adding to find the answer.	**Before:** Remind the children of the strategy of combining the multiplication of the tens digit with the multiplication of the units digit to find the answer. **After:** Mark the homework together and check that the children have understood the strategy.	10	205
Where does it fit?	● Compare familiar fractions: for example, know that on the number line one half lies between one quarter and three quarters.	**Maths homework** Comparing fractions and ordering them onto a number line.	**Before:** Draw a number line labelled 0 to 1 and ask the children to place fractions such as 1/2 and 3/4 onto it. **After:** Mark the homework together and check that the children can order fractions on a number line with reasonable accuracy.	11	209

NNS OBJECTIVES — Teacher's notes

Activity name	Learning objectives	Content of homework	Managing the homework	All New 100 Maths Lessons Year 3	
				NNS	Page
Fraction estimate	● Estimate a simple fraction.	**Maths to share** Estimating fractions of measures.	**Before:** Remind the children that measures can be seen as fractions of the whole unit, for example nearly 50cm is about 1/2 a metre. **After:** Review the homework together. Ask the children which questions they found most difficult and why, and discuss the answers so that all understand.	11	211
Money totals	● Extend understanding that more than two numbers can be added: add three or four two-digit numbers with the help of apparatus or pencil and paper.	**Maths homework** Finding the total price of three items, with each price less than £1.	**Before:** Discuss how several amounts of money can be totalled, by, for example, looking for pairs to make £1. **After:** Discuss the addition sentences that the children made and the strategies that they used for totalling.	12	214
Column addition	● Use informal pencil-and-paper methods to support, record or explain HTU ± TU and HTU ± HTU.	**Maths homework** Using a column method to total HTU + TU.	**Before:** Remind the children of the school's method for column addition. **After:** Mark the homework together. Invite individual children to demonstrate on the board how they worked out the answer.	12	215
Bar charts	● **Solve a given problem by organising and interpreting numerical data in simple lists, tables, and graphs,** for example: bar charts – intervals labelled in ones then twos.	**Maths homework** Interpreting data in a bar chart with intervals labelled in twos.	**Before:** Ask the children to look carefully at the bar chart on the homework sheet and to say what its scale is. **After:** Mark the homework together, asking children from each ability group to give answers.	13	221

Name

Date

Number order

■ Write these sets of numbers in order, starting with the smallest, on the empty number line.

■ See how quickly you can do this.

165 156 651 615 516 561

831 901 879 910 887 897

501 516 499 504 497 500

222 213 201 202 231 200

■ Now choose three of these digits each time and make a three-digit number: 4 8 5 9

■ Write the number in the boxes below.

■ Do this three more times on the back of the sheet. Write the numbers in order.

Dear Helper

This activity helps your child to order three-digit numbers. If your child is unsure of how to begin, ask them to look at the hundreds digits first. They can then find the lowest of these, or maybe two which are the same. Now ask them to look at the tens digits and find the lowest of these, and finally the units digit. This will help them to order the numbers, smallest to largest. Challenge your child to choose any three digits, make as many three-digit numbers as they can from these, and position them, in order, onto a number line.

PHOTOCOPIABLE

Name

Date

Adding and adjusting

◢ Choose a number from the first grid.

◢ Add 19, 21, 29 or 31 to it.

◢ See if you can find your answer in the second grid. If it is there, put a cross through it.

◢ Repeat this until all the numbers in the second grid have been crossed out.

45	65	56	57	52
34	69	28	29	62

75	58	64	49	73
86	86	63	100	81

Dear Helper

This activity helps your child to use the strategy of adding the closest multiple of 10 and adjusting by 1. So, for 45 + 19 this would be 45 + 20 – 1. If your child is unsure about how to begin, suggest that they begin with the first number, 45, and try adding 19, 21, and so on until they find the answer in the second grid. Discuss their addition strategy, and, if this will help, suggest that your child writes out the number sentence of 45 + 19 = 45 + 20 – 1 until they are confident with using this strategy. As a further challenge, ask your child to make up a similar puzzle to try with their friends back at school.

www.scholastic.co.uk

Number patterns

- Write the answers to these number sentences.
- Continue the patterns.

16 + 8 = ☐	97 − 7 = ☐	24 + 7 = ☐	93 − 7 = ☐
16 + 18 = ☐	97 − 17 = ☐	24 + 17 = ☐	93 − 17 = ☐
16 + 28 = ☐	97 − 27 = ☐	24 + 27 = ☐	93 − 27 = ☐
16 + ☐ = ☐	97 − ☐ = ☐	24 + ☐ = ☐	93 − ☐ = ☐
16 + ☐ = ☐	97 − ☐ = ☐	24 + ☐ = ☐	93 − ☐ = ☐
16 + ☐ = ☐	97 − ☐ = ☐	24 + ☐ = ☐	93 − ☐ = ☐
16 + ☐ = ☐	97 − ☐ = ☐	24 + ☐ = ☐	93 − ☐ = ☐
16 + ☐ = ☐	97 − ☐ = ☐	24 + ☐ = ☐	93 − ☐ = ☐
16 + ☐ = ☐	97 − ☐ = ☐	24 + ☐ = ☐	93 − ☐ = ☐

Dear Helper
This activity helps your child to spot addition and subtraction patterns and to use these to help them to calculate. If your child is unsure, discuss what is happening. For example, if 16 + 8 = 24, then what is 16 + 18, 16 + 28, and so on. Discuss how the answer increases by 10 each time, as does the number that is added to 16. For the subtraction patterns, ask your child to explain what happens each time (reduces by 10 each time). Challenge your child to write their own add and subtract patterns.

Name

Date

Add and subtract

■ Use the empty number line to help you to find the answers to these addition and subtraction sentences.

45 + 36 = ☐

65 – 28 = ☐

84 + 68 = ☐

84 – 67 = ☐

93 + 78 = ☐

91 – 56 = ☐

121 + 59 = ☐

123 – 35 = ☐

145 + 92 = ☐

342 – 97 = ☐

Dear Helper

This activity encourages your child to use an informal pencil-and-paper method, before they are introduced to more formal methods in the next school year. If your child is unsure about how to start, for the addition, ask them to write the larger number onto the empty number line, then to count up in tens and then units until they reach the second number.

They should mark the steps on the line, as shown *right*. For subtraction, ask your child to write the number to be taken away onto the number line, then to count up to the

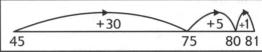

second number like this: To calculate 65 – 28: 28 and 2 to 30; 30 and 30 to 60; and 5 more to 65. So 65 – 28 = 2 + 30 + 5 = 37. Challenge your child to do these questions as quickly and accurately as they can.

PHOTOCOPIABLE

www.scholastic.co.uk

Name	Date

How much? (1)

- ◼ Write the answer to each problem.
- ◼ There is space for jottings.
- ◼ Now write a check calculation to check your answer.

Problem and answer	Jottings	Check calculation
Jasmine buys some fruit for her class. There are 25 children in the class and each child has two pieces of fruit. There are 12 pieces of fruit left over. How many pieces of fruit did Jasmine buy?		
Peter helps his mum to wash the dishes every evening. He spends nine minutes each evening doing this. How long does he spend washing dishes during one week? minutes		
Sarah always brings an apple to school to eat at break. In July there were only three whole weeks and three days at school. So how many apples did she need?		

Dear Helper

This activity helps your child to decide which mathematics to use, and then to check with an equivalent calculation. If your child finds this difficult, talk through the problem. Decide what the question is asking, and which information is needed to solve the problem. Discuss which mathematics to use. To check, ask your child to suggest another way of working out the problem. Challenge your child to find more than one way to check each problem's answer.

Measuring bonanza

◗ Decide how to measure the capacity of each of these.

◗ Tick the correct box.

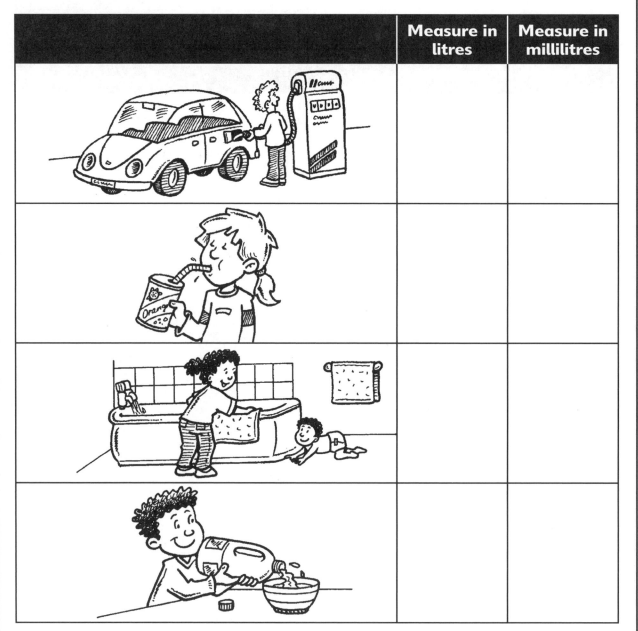

	Measure in litres	Measure in millilitres

◗ Now look around you at home. Make lists of things measured in millimetres and things measured in litres on the back of this sheet.

Dear Helper

This activity helps your child to recognise which units would be best to measure capacity in each situation in the pictures. Discuss each picture with your child and encourage them to come to a decision about which would be best, and to explain why. In addition to the second part, you could challenge your child to write a list of things outside the home measured in litres.

Name

Date

How much? (2)

■ Write how much is in each container.

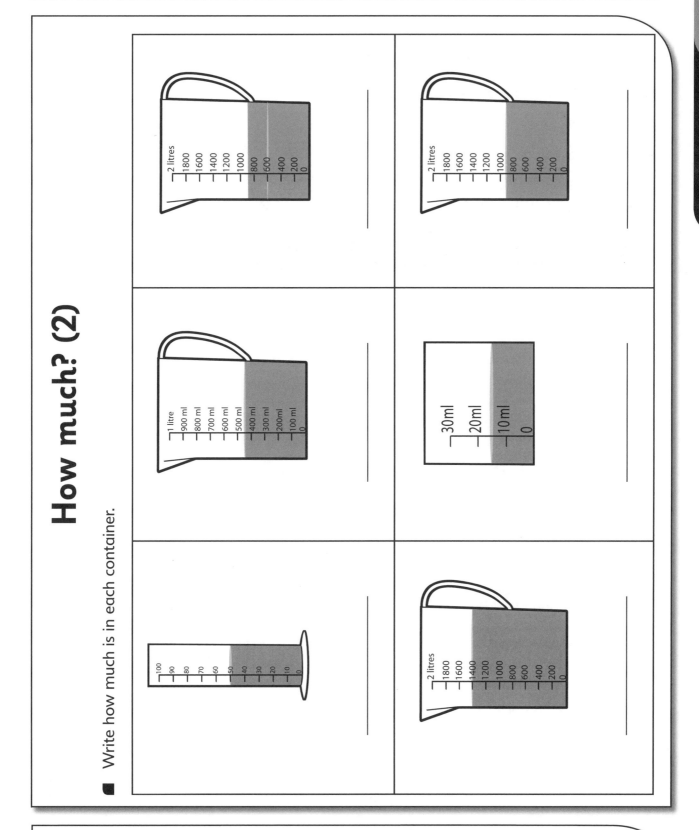

Dear Helper

This activity helps your child to read scales marked in millilitres and litres. If your child is unsure about how to read these, ask them to say how the scale is marked, what the start mark is, and how the scale increases. Ask them to look at the closest mark to the level of the liquid and to read this, then to make any adjustment if the liquid is above this. Challenge your child to fill a litre jug marked in millilitres to the level that you say.

Name

Date

Measures word problems

◢ Decide how to solve each problem.

◢ Write the answer.

◢ Write how you solved it:

M for mental calculation **MJ** for mental and jottings **P** for pencil-and-paper method

Problem	Answer	Method
There is 1 litre and 400ml left in the milk bottle. Jan drinks 500ml of the milk. How much is left now?		
A bag of apples weighs 450 grams. A bag of pears weighs twice as much as the apples. How much do the apples and pears weigh in total?		
There are 50 metres of ribbon on the reel. Marcie buys 14 metres of the ribbon and Jane buys $18\frac{1}{2}$ metres. How much ribbon is left on the reel now?		
The film at the cinema starts at 7.30pm. It finishes at 9.45pm. How long does the film last?		

Dear Helper

This activity helps your child to make decisions about how to solve problems. Discuss with your child which way they will solve each problem: mentally, mentally with some jottings, or a paper-and-pencil method such as using an empty number line. Discuss how to record the answer. For the first question, for example, the answer could be recorded in millilitres, as a fraction of a litre or as a decimal fraction of a litre. You could challenge your child to record their answer in at least two different ways.

PHOTOCOPIABLE

Name	Date

Is it symmetrical?

◼ Look carefully at each shape.

◼ Put a cross through the shapes that have no lines of symmetry.

◼ Draw in the lines of symmetry in the other shapes.

☐ Hint: some shapes have one line of symmetry, some shapes have more than one.

☐ Use a mirror if you are unsure.

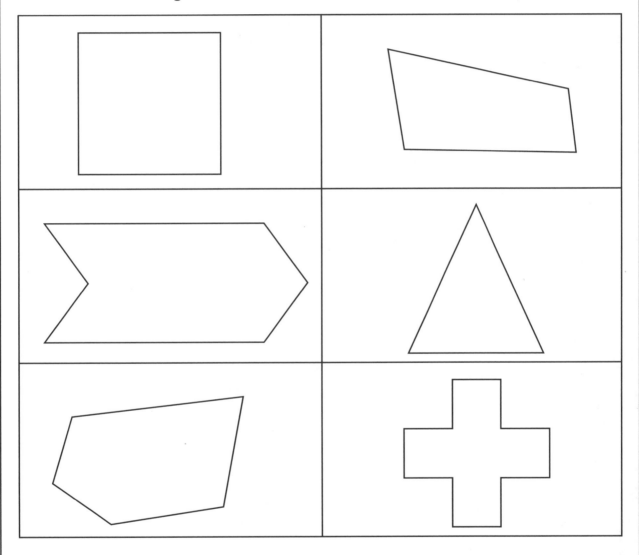

Dear Helper

This activity helps your child to recognise which shapes have lines of symmetry and where the symmetry is. If your child finds this difficult, provide a small hand mirror and ask them to place the mirror on one half of the shape, with the mirror standing vertically, so that they can see the shape reflected. By repositioning the mirror the child can check where lines of symmetry are, and check to see which shapes have no symmetry. Challenge your child to draw their own symmetrical shapes and to mark in the lines of symmetry.

PHOTOCOPIABLE

www.scholastic.co.uk

Name _____   Date _____

What's my shape?

■ Read the description of each shape.

■ Write the name of the shape and sketch a picture of it.

I am a 2-D shape. I have four straight sides. I have no right angles. What am I? _____	I am a 3-D shape. I have one flat face. I have one curved face. My flat face is circular. What am I? _____
I am a 2-D shape. I have one right angle. My three sides are straight. What am I? _____	I am a 3-D shape. I have four flat faces which are triangles. I have one flat face which has four sides the same length and all angles are right angles. What am I? _____
I am a 3-D shape. I have one flat face. I have one curved face which meets at a vertex. What am I? _____	I am a 2-D shape. I have five equal angles. I have five sides all the same length. What am I? _____

Dear Helper
This activity helps your child to use general statements about shapes. If your child finds this difficult, read together each line of the description and decide what shapes this could refer to and what shapes do not fit. Challenge your child to write their own general description of a regular shape.

PHOTOCOPIABLE

www.scholastic.co.uk

Multiples of 2, 5 and 10

◖ See how quickly you can do this. Time how long it takes.

◖ Circle the multiples of 2.

| 1 | 4 | 9 | 18 | 36 | 45 | 88 | 102 | 654 | 748 |

◖ Circle the multiples of 5.

| 5 | 12 | 25 | 41 | 52 | 65 | 80 | 315 | 450 | 900 |

◖ Circle the multiples of 10.

| 9 | 20 | 47 | 80 | 95 | 100 | 120 | 231 | 845 | 870 |

◖ Write the list of unit digits that tell you that a number is a multiple of 2.

_____

◖ Write the list of unit digits that tell you that a number is a multiple of 5.

_____

◖ Write how you can tell that a number is a multiple of 10.

_____

_____

◖ Write three numbers which are each a multiple of 2, 5 and 10.

_____

◖ I took ☐ minutes to do this.

Dear Helper

This activity helps your child to use the rules for recognising multiples of 2, 5 and 10. If your child is unsure, take each number in the list at a time, and ask your child to decide whether it will come in the count of 2s... 5s... 10s... Challenge your child to write a list of numbers that are not multiples of 2, 5 or 10.

Multiples of 50 and 100

■ Look at these numbers.

■ Join the multiples of 50 to the fifty.

■ Join the multiples of 100 to the hundred.

■ Circle the numbers that are neither multiples of 50 nor multiples of 100.

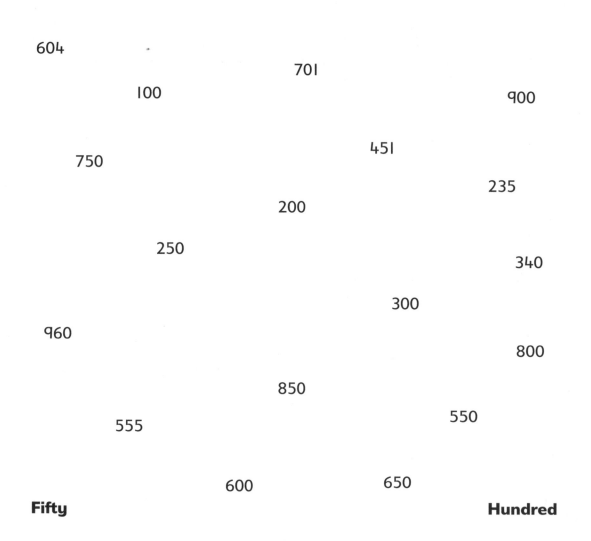

604

701

100

900

451

750

235

200

250

340

300

960

800

850

550

555

600   650

Fifty   **Hundred**

Dear Helper
This activity helps your child to use the rules for recognising multiples of 50 and 100. If your child is unsure, take each number at a time, and ask your child to decide whether it will come in the count of 50 or 100. Discuss how to recognise multiples of 50 (end in 50 or 00) and 100 (end in 00). You could challenge your child to write a list of numbers, larger than 100, that are multiples of 50 or 100.

PHOTOCOPIABLE

www.scholastic.co.uk

Remainder search

- Here are 24 ladybirds.
- Divide the ladybirds by 2, 3, 4, 5 and 10.
- Find which numbers give remainders.
- Record using the number sentences.

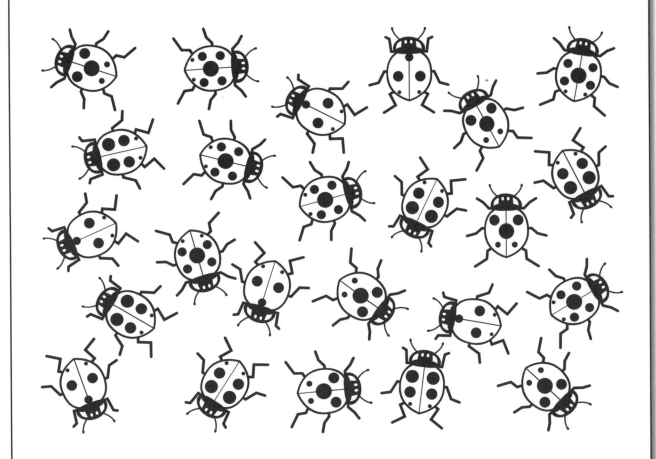

24 ÷ 2 = _____   24 ÷ 3 = _____

24 ÷ 4 = _____   24 ÷ 5 = _____

24 ÷ 10 = _____

Dear Helper

This activity helps your child to use the multiplication table facts that they know to find division facts, and to identify where there is a remainder. If your child is unsure, say the appropriate multiplication table together until either the appropriate fact is found, or the nearest fact, then discuss what is 'left over', which will make the remainder. If your child would enjoy the challenge, ask them to divide 24 by 6, 7, 8 and 9 to see where there will be a remainder.

PHOTOCOPIABLE

Name   Date

Division problems

- Write the answers to these questions.

- Remember to think about whether you need to round up or down to find the answer.

- There is room to make jottings.

There are 34 children in Class 3. Each child needs a new jotter. Jotters come in packs of ten.	The children in Class 3 have been invited to a party. They will travel there in cars. Each car will hold four passengers.
How many packs are needed? ☐	How many cars are needed? ☐
The children in Class 3 have been invited to the cinema. Tickets come in books of six at £5 a book.	The school buys apples to sell at playtime. The apples are put out in baskets, with ten apples in each basket. There are 54 apples.
How many ticket books are needed? ☐ How much does this cost? ☐	How many baskets can be filled? ☐

Dear Helper

This activity helps your child to use multiplication facts to find division facts, and to decide whether to round the answer up or down, depending on the question. Ask your child to read the question with you, and decide whether the answer will round up or down. If your child is unsure about this, talk about the division and whether there is a remainder and how to deal with this for this question. Challenge your child to complete the questions as quickly and accurately as they can.

Name

Date

Multiplying and dividing by 10 and 100

◼ Write the answers to these questions.

◼ See how quickly you can do this. Time how long it takes.

3 x 10 = ☐

7 x 100 = ☐

25 x 10 = ☐

5 x 100 = ☐

60 ÷ 10 = ☐

500 ÷ 100 = ☐

800 ÷ 10 = ☐

900 ÷ 100 = ☐

40 ÷ 10 = ☐

8 x 100 = ☐

I took ☐ minutes to do this.

Dear Helper

This activity helps your child to recognise that when multiplying by 10 the digits shift one place to the left and when mulitplying by 100 they shift two places to the left. When dividing by 10 the digits shift one place to the right; when dividing by 100 they shift two places to the right. If your child is unsure, discuss whether it is a division or multiplication question and which way the digits will shift. Challenge your child to work quickly and accurately.

PHOTOCOPIABLE

Name _____   Date _____

Tens and units multiplication

■ This is a way to calculate 32 x 2.

30 x 2 = 60

2 x 2 = 4

So 32 x 2 = 60 + 4 = 64

■ Now try this method for these multiplication sentences.

43 x 2	23 x 2
24 x 3	48 x 2
14 x 3	26 x 4

Dear Helper

This activity helps your child to use a method for multiplication of tens and units by units. If your child is unsure, follow the example given above and work through each question, multiplying the tens digit first, then the units, then combine the two to find the answer. To extend the activity, challenge your child to write five more of these questions for themselves and see how quickly they can find the answer.

Name	Date

Where does it fit?

■ Decide where these fractions will fit onto the number line.

$\dfrac{1}{2}$ $\dfrac{1}{4}$ $\dfrac{1}{8}$

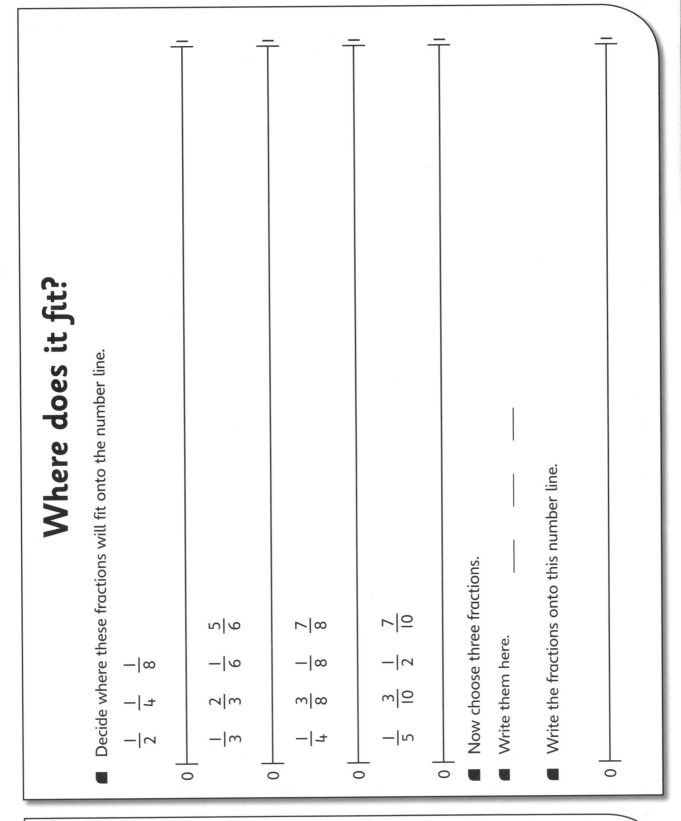

$\dfrac{1}{3}$ $\dfrac{2}{3}$ $\dfrac{1}{6}$ $\dfrac{5}{6}$

$\dfrac{1}{4}$ $\dfrac{3}{8}$ $\dfrac{1}{8}$ $\dfrac{7}{8}$

$\dfrac{1}{5}$ $\dfrac{3}{10}$ $\dfrac{1}{2}$ $\dfrac{7}{10}$

■ Now choose three fractions.

■ Write them here. — — —

■ Write the fractions onto this number line.

Dear Helper
This activity helps your child to compare and order fractions, placing them in order on a number line. If your child is unsure, compare two of the fractions and ask your child to decide which is larger and which is smaller, and why they think that. They can then compare other pairs in the set in the same way. Challenge your child to choose another set of three fractions and to position these, in order, onto a number line.

Fraction estimate

■ Estimate and write the fraction that you can see.

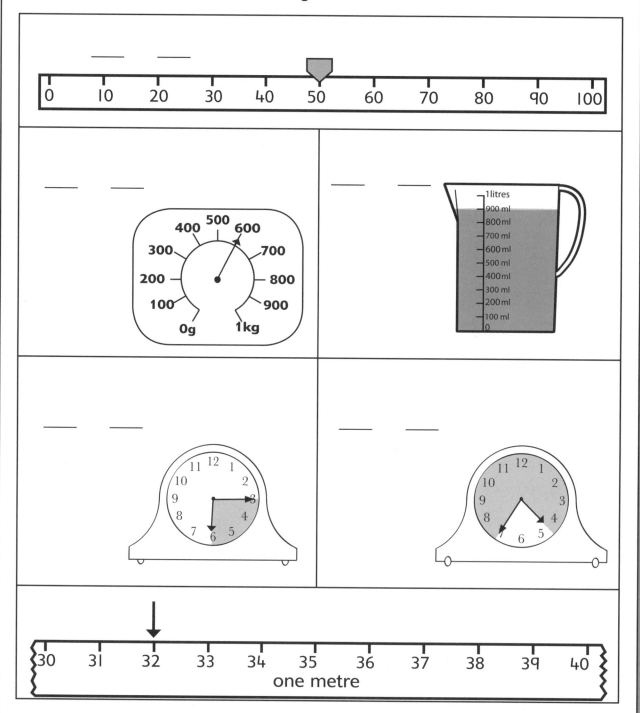

Dear Helper

This activity helps your child to make estimates using fractions. If your child is unsure, discuss what they can see in the picture, and where the reading is. Discuss which the closest reading is, then compare this with the whole. So, for example, the first one reads nearly 50cm, which is ½ of a metre. Challenge your child to complete these quickly and accurately.

ALL NEW 100 MATHS HOMEWORK AND ASSESSMENT · YEAR 3

www.scholastic.co.uk

Money totals

- Choose three of these items from the shop.

- Find the total each time.

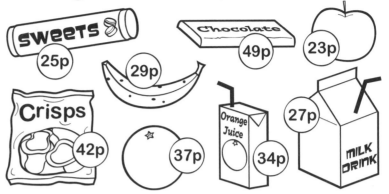

sweets 25p

29p

Chocolate 49p

23p

Crisps 42p

37p

Orange Juice 34p

27p

MILK DRINK

I chose: _____

_____

_____

This cost _____

I chose: _____

_____

_____

This cost _____

I chose: _____

_____

_____

This cost _____

I chose: _____

_____

_____

This cost _____

Dear Helper

This activity helps your child to choose strategies for totalling two-digit numbers. If necessary, remind your child to record their answer in pounds – 145 pence is the same as £1.45. If your child needs further help with this, provide some coins to help them. Extend this activity by challenging your child to total four or five prices each time.

PHOTOCOPIABLE

Name   Date

Column addition

◼ Work out the answers to these questions using two different methods.

◼ Use a horizontal method first.

◼ Now use the column addition method that you were taught at school.

◼ Write the answer.

◼ Check that both methods give the same answer.

246 + 87 = ☐	2 4 6 + 8 7
545 + 78 = ☐	5 4 5 + 7 8
298 + 79 = ☐	2 9 8 + 7 9

Dear Helper

Your child has been taught a method of column addition at school. Ask your child to explain this to you. It may not be the method that you were taught, but please help your child to do these in the way that they have been taught at school. By working out each question using two different methods of setting out the addition sentence, your child is learning that both methods give the same answer, and that the way of working is similar. Challenge your child to do these quickly and efficiently.

PHOTOCOPIABLE

www.scholastic.co.uk

Name	Date

Bar charts

◼ Use the bar chart to help you to answer the questions.

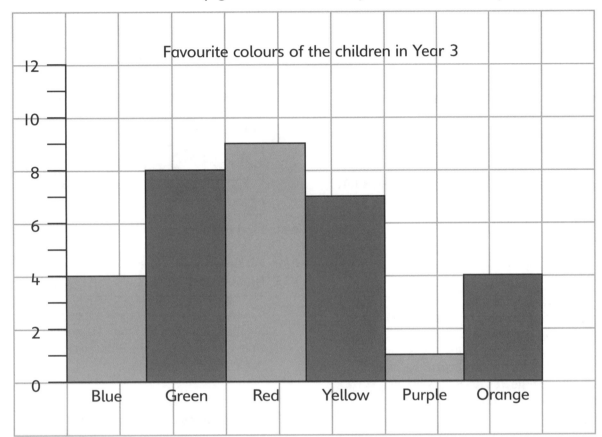

Favourite colours of the children in Year 3

◼ How many more children liked red than purple? _____

◼ Which was the most popular colour? _____

◼ Every child in Year 3 decided on their favourite
colour. How many children are there in Year 3? _____

◼ Which was the least popular colour? _____

◼ What is your favourite colour? _____

Dear Helper
This activity helps your child to interpret data in a bar chart where the intervals are labelled in twos.
This means that every square represents two children in this chart. If your child is unsure about the
scale, count up the green column in twos to see how many there are. Do this again for the red column
and discuss how the red is halfway between 8 and 10. Challenge your child to find some data about
the family and draw a bar chart for this, with a scale of one square representing two things.

Answer sheet

Autumn term

P13 Number match Answers for the second part will vary.

P14 Partitioning 600, 40, 9; 300, 30, 3; 500, 0, 9; 500, 90, 0; 900, 50, 0; 900, 0, 5; 200, 30, 7. Answers for the second part will vary.

P15 Addition 55; 84; 69; 79; 88; 93; 51; 97; 83; 101.

P16 Money puzzle The different combinations are: 20p + 20p + 20p = 60p; 20p + 20p + 50p = 90p; 20p + 50p + 50p = £1.20; 50p + 50p + 50p = £1.50; 20p + 20p + £1 = £1.40; 20p + £1 + £1 = £2.20; £1 + £1 + £1 = £3; 20p + 20p + £2 = £2.40; 20p + £2 + £2 = £4.20; £2 + £2 + £2 = £6; 50p + 50p + £1 = £2; 50p + £1 + £1 = £2.50; 50p + 50p + £2 = £3; 50p + £2 + £2 = £4.50; £1 + £1 + £2 = £4; £1 + £2 + £2 = £5; £1 + 20p + 50p = £1.70; 20p + 50p + £2 = £2.70; £2 + 50p + £1 = £3.50; £2 + £1 + 20p = £3.20.

P17 Telling the time *6.10; 5.25; 9.15; 7.20; 8.50; 3.35; 4.55; 12.00; 10.40; 2.45.* Answers for the second part will vary.

P18 10 centimetres Answers will vary.

P19 Sorting 2-D shapes

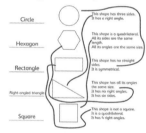

P20 Holiday map Check the coordinates given against the grid.

P21 Is it true? The sentence 'All squares are rectangles' is true. Answers will vary.

P22 Odd numbers Answers will vary.

P23 Odds and evens Answers will vary.

P24 Estimating Answers will vary.

P25 Multiplication arrays

4 x 2 = 8; 4 + 4 = 8; 2 + 2 + 2 + 2 = 8.

5 x 4 = 20; 5 + 5 + 5 + 5 = 20; 4 + 4 + 4 + 4 + 4 = 20.

6 x 3 = 18; 6 + 6 + 6 = 18; 3 + 3 + 3 + 3 + 3 + 3 = 18.

7 x 3 = 21; 7 + 7 + 7 = 21; 3 + 3 + 3 + 3 + 3 + 3 + 3 = 21.

P26 Times 10 and 100 50, 500; 80, 800; 40, 400; 90, 900; 70, 700; 10, 100; 100, 1000; 300, 3000; 800, 8000; 900, 9000.

P27 Find the change 20p – 16p = 4p; 50p – 16p = 34p; £1 – 16p = 84p; £2 – 16p = £1.84.

P28 Presents Answers will vary.

P29 Fraction search Cake 1/2; Pizza 1/3; Chocolate 1/10; Paper 1/4; Apples 1/8.

P30 Fraction shade

$\frac{1}{2}$ or $\frac{2}{4}$		$\frac{3}{5}$		$\frac{2}{5}$	$\frac{3}{4}$
$\frac{3}{9}$ or $\frac{1}{3}$		$\frac{7}{8}$		$\frac{7}{10}$	$\frac{3}{10}$

P31 Find the difference 3; 6; 4; 6; 6; 5; 5; 7; 9; 4.

P32 My time Answers will vary.

P33 Number sort Answers will vary. Possible sortings include: odd numbers and not odd numbers; even numbers and not even numbers; numbers less than 10, not less than 10; numbers in the 3 times-table and not in the 3 times-table.

Spring term

P38 Number compare Answers will vary.

P39 Race track challenge Answers will vary.

P40 Add these 24; 25; 26; 32; 37; 33; 37; 41; 41; 36. Answers to the second part will vary.

P41 Sticker problems 65; 50; 40; 57; 57.

P42 Check it 64; 76; 37; 29; 30; 87; 97; 36; 49; 87.

P43 Find it! Answers to all three parts will vary.

P44 Making shapes

Cutting one right angle:

Cutting two right angles:

P45 What's the time?

P46 **How heavy?** 550g; 1.5kg; 3kg.

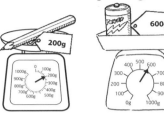 

P47 **What's the problem?** 51; 8 r2; 4; 9. Answers to the second part will vary.

P48 **Counting patterns** Answers will vary.

P49 **Number square challenge** Answers will vary.

P50 **Division hops** 8; 6; 7; 6; 8; 3.

P51 **Double and halve** Part 1: 30, 15; 28, 14; 18, 9; 36, 18; 32, 16. Part 2: 24, 12; 26, 13; 34, 17; 38, 19. Answers to the third part will vary.

P52 **Multiplication and division** 5 x 4 = 20, 4 x 5 = 20, 20 ÷ 5 = 4, 20 ÷ 4 = 5; 6 x 3 = 18, 3 x 6 = 18, 18 ÷ 3 = 6, 18 ÷ 6 = 3; 8 x 3 = 24, 3 x 8 = 24, 24 ÷ 3 = 8, 24 ÷ 8 = 3; 6 x 5 = 30, 5 x 6 = 30, 30 ÷ 5 = 6, 30 ÷ 6 = 5; 9 x 10 = 90, 10 x 9 = 90, 90 ÷ 9 = 10, 90 ÷ 10 = 9.

P53 **Calculation check** 71; 7; 5; 32; 19.

P54 **Fraction shade** 2/8,1/4; 4/10, 2/5; 4/6, 2/3; 8/10, 4/5; 5/10, 1/2.

P55 **Fraction match** No answers.

P56 **Venn diagram sort** Is a multiple of 5: 20, 25, 30, 35, 40, 45, 50; all remaining numbers are not a multiple of 5. Is a multiple of 3: 21, 24, 27, 30, 33, 36, 39, 42, 45, 48; all remaining numbers are not a multiple of 3.

Summer term

P61 **Number order** 156, 165, 516, 561, 615, 651; 831, 879, 887, 897, 901, 910; 497, 499, 500, 501, 504, 516; 200, 201, 202, 213, 222, 231. Answers to the second part will vary.

P62 **Adding and adjusting** 45 (+ 19) 64; 65 (+ 21) 86; 56 (+ 19) 75; 57 (+ 29) 86; 52 (+ 21) 73; 34 (+ 29) 63; 69 (+ 31) 100; 28 (+ 21) 49; 29 (+ 29) 58; 62 (+ 19) 81.

P63 **Number patterns** 16 + 8 = 24, 16 + 18 = 34, 16 + 28 = 44, 16 + 38 = 54, 16 + 48 = 64, 16 + 58 = 74, 16 + 68 = 84, 16 + 78 = 94, 16 + 88 = 104; 97 – 7 = 90, 97 – 17 = 80, 97 – 27 = 70, 97 – 37 = 60, 97 – 47 = 50, 97 – 57 = 40, 97 – 67 = 30, 97 – 77 = 20, 97 – 87 = 10; 24 + 7 = 31, 24 + 17 = 41, 24 + 27 = 51, 24 + 37 = 61, 24 + 47 = 71, 24 + 57 = 81, 24 + 67 = 91, 24 + 77 = 101, 24 + 87 = 111; 93 – 7 = 86, 93 – 17 = 76, 93 + 27 = 66, 93 – 37 = 56, 93 – 47 = 46, 93 – 57 = 36, 93 – 67 = 26, 93 – 77 = 16, 93 – 87 = 6.

P64 **Add and subtract** 81, 152, 171, 180, 237, 37, 17, 35, 88, 245.

P65 **How much? (1)** 62; 63; 18.

P66 **Measuring bonanza** litres; millilitres; litres; millilitres. Answers to the second part will vary.

P67 **How much? (2)** 50ml; 450ml; 600ml or 6/10 litre or 0.6 litre; 1 litre 400ml or 1.4 litre; 15ml; 900ml or 9/10 litre or 0.9 litre.

P68 **Measures word problems** 900ml or 0.9 litres or 9/10 litre; 1350 grams or 1.35 kilograms or 1 kilogram 350 grams; 17½ metres or 17.5 metres or 17 metres and 50 centimetres; 2¼ hours or 2 hours 15 minutes.

P69 **Is it symmetrical?** Lines of symmetry: The other shapes have no lines of symmetry.

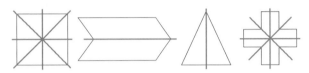

P70 **What's my shape?** Quadrilateral; Right-angled triangle; Cone; Hemisphere (or cone or half ellipsoid); (square) Pyramid; Pentagon.

P71 **Multiples of 2, 5 and 10** 4, 18, 36, 88, 102, 654, 748; 5, 25, 65, 80, 315, 450, 900; 20, 80, 100, 120, 870; 0, 2, 4, 6, 8; 0, 5; Has 0 as its unit digit; Any number with 0 as its digit.

P72 **Multiples of 50 and 100** Multiples of 50: 100, 200, 250, 300, 550, 600, 650, 750, 800, 850, 900; Multiples of 100; 100, 200, 300, 600, 800, 900. Numbers to be circled: 235, 340, 451, 555, 604, 701, 960.

P73 **Remainder search** 12; 8; 6; 4 r4; 2 r4.

P74 **Division problems** 4; 9; 6, £30; 5.

P75 **Multiplying and dividing by 10 and 100** 30; 700; 250; 500; 6; 5; 80; 9; 4; 800.

P76 **Tens and units multiplication** 86; 46; 72; 96; 42; 104.

P77 **Where does it fit?**

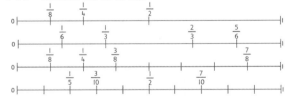

P78 **Fraction estimate** 1/2; 6/10 or 3/5; 9/10; 1/4; 2/3; 2/10 or 1/5.

P79 **Money totals** Answers will vary.

P80 **Column addition** 333; 623; 377.

P81 **Bar charts** 8; red; 33; purple. Answers to the fifth part will vary.

Year 3 Key objectives
Below is the complete list of key objectives covered in Year 3. The letters alongside each objective also appear alongside each assessment activity. This will help you to identify which objectives are covered by each activity.

a Read, write and order whole numbers to at least 1000; know what each digit represents.

b Count on or back in tens or hundreds from any two- or three-digit number.

c Recognise unit fractions such as 1/2, 1/3, 1/4, 1/5, 1/10, and use them to find fractions of shapes and numbers.

d Know by heart all addition and subtraction facts for each number to 20.

e Add and subtract mentally a 'near multiple of 10' to or from a two-digit number.

f Know by heart facts for the 2, 5 and 10 multiplication tables.

g Understand division and recognise that division is the inverse of multiplication.

h Use units of time and know the relationships between them (second, minute, hour, day, week, month, year).

i Understand and use £.p notation.

j Choose and use appropriate operations (including multiplication and division) to solve word problems, explaining methods and reasoning.

k Identify right angles.

l Identify lines of symmetry in simple shapes and recognise shapes with no lines of symmetry.

m Solve a given problem by organising and interpreting numerical data in simple lists, tables and graphs.

Introduction
The planning for the assessment units is based upon the NNS medium-term plans. There is an assessment unit for each end of half-term, as well as end-of-year assessments. Each unit consists of two detailed lesson plans, each assessing one of the key objectives, with an accompanying photocopiable activity sheet for each lesson. The notes include suggestions for further work where children have not met the objective. There are additional oral and mental, practical and written activities covering the range of key objectives taught that half-term, with photocopiable assessment sheets for written work. For the end-of-year assessment there are mental and written tests covering all the Year 3 key objectives. The end-of-year assessments mirror the style of the national tests or QCA non-statutory tests. Further information about the end-of-year assessments is provided on page 133.

Using the assessment units
Choose the half-term assessment that matches your planning needs. From your ongoing teacher assessments, identify the children that you believe have achieved specific key objectives. Now decide upon the children who you suspect may have met the key objectives but for whom you have no firm assessment data (a class record sheet has been provided on page 141 for this purpose). These children can form the target group for assessment. Arrange for them to work with an adult during practical activities. The adult should use the probing questions included in the assessment notes for teachers. Ask all the children to complete the written assessments, putting the probing questions to the targeted group.

Supporting teaching assistants
Provide the teaching assistant with details of the activity (whether practical or written). Discuss the probing questions to be used and how responses will be recorded. Did the child give appropriate, correct responses to the questions? Was a specific question answered inappropriately? Where the latter occurs, some additional notes about what the child failed to understand would be helpful for planning future teaching. Discuss the outcomes of the assessment activity together and make notes about individual children.

Assessment for learning
Assessment is always for a purpose – here it is to check what individual children understand, know and can do, and where they need further teaching in order to achieve the key objectives. Use the outcomes of the assessment for forward planning for teaching and for homework provision. The *All New 100 Maths Lessons* series provides detailed planning grids for each term, which can be used to identify further activities to support those who need more experiences in particular topics.

Assess and Review

Key objectives to be assessed
Assessment lesson 1: **Understand and use £.p notation**
Assessment lesson 2: **Identify right angles**

Photocopiable pages
Money (p87); Right angles (p89); Money and word problems (p90); Assessment test (pages 91-92).

Equipment
Individual whiteboards and pens; sheets of A4 paper; mixed coins; 2-D shapes tiles with and without right angles; Blu-Tack.

Assessment Activities

Mental maths assessment
Two- and three-digit numbers ⓐ
Explain that you will say a two- or three-digit number. Ask the children to write this on their whiteboards, and, when you say 'Show me', hold up their boards for you to see. Begin with two-digit numbers, then move to three-digit numbers.
Probing questions
● *In the number 203, what does the 2/0/3 represent?*
● *Write another number using the digits 0, 2, 3. What have you written? What does the 0/2/3 represent now?*

Practical maths assessment
Finding right angles ⓚ
Ask the children to fold a sheet of A4 paper into quarters, in order to make a fairly rigid right angle. Ask them to spend about five minutes moving around the classroom and to find items with a right angle, such as the corner of the front cover of a book or a window pane. Ask them to list the things they choose, and to make another list of things that do not have a right angle.
Probing questions
● *What do you look for when checking whether a vertex (corner or angle) is a right angle?*
● *Think of something at home that has a right angle. What did you think of?*

Written maths assessment
Provide copies of the assessment sheet 'Money and word problems'. Either ask all the children in the class to complete this sheet and then ask the probing questions listed below of a group you wish to assess, or work with a targeted group and use the probing questions as the children work. Check that the children understand what to do for each part of the sheet.
Probing questions
As they work, ask of individuals:

● *How many pennies is £2.49?*
● *Tell me another way to write 650 pence.*

● *How did you know whether to choose addition/ subtraction/multiplication/division to solve this problem?*
● *Make up a word problem which uses this calculation: 4 x 5.*
● *What are the important things to remember when solving word problems?*

Money

> **Key objective:**
> **Understand and use £.p notation.**

> **What you need**
> ● A pot of mixed coins for each pair of children; a copy of the 'Money' assessment sheet for each child.

> **Further support**
> Consider limiting the amounts of money to £1 or £2, and alter the assessment sheet if necessary. The children can work as a larger group with an adult. The adult should encourage each child to find a way of making the amount of money and record them all on the flipchart. Then the children can decide which way uses the least number of coins, with the adult's help.

Oral and mental starter

Explain that you have a coin hidden. Encourage the children to ask questions about the hidden coin until someone guesses what it is. Children can ask questions such as: *Is it silver/bronze/gold? Is it worth more than/less than...?* You must answer yes or no to the questions. When the children are confident with this, ask a child to choose a coin, hide it, then answer yes or no to questions asked by the rest of the class.

Main assessment activity

Explain that in this lesson you want to find out how well the children can change pence into pounds and pence, and find the least number of coins to make an amount of money. Provide each pair with a pot of mixed coins. Say: *Find a way to make 120 pence. Use the least number of coins that you can.* When the children have done this, ask one of them to write 120 pence on the board using £.p notation: £1.20. Discuss which coins the children have chosen. The least here is £1 and 20p. Repeat this for another amount of money, such as 245p.

When the children are confident with this activity, provide a copy of the 'Money' assessment sheet for each child. Ask them to take turns to choose an amount of money, and to say it in pennies. They should write the amount in pence, in pounds and pence, and write the least number of coins they can use to make that amount.

Plenary

Repeat the activity with the whole class. This time ask the children to work in pairs and to each find a different way of making up the amount of money using coins. However, remind them that all of it in pennies may be too heavy to handle! Give the children a couple of minutes to do this. Now invite children from each ability group to write up how they made up the amount of money. Repeat this for another amount, such as £2.50, £3.85 or £1.75. Ask questions such as:

● *How would you order these amounts of money, starting with the largest/ smallest?*

● *Write down 15p, £1.50, £15. What do you notice about how these are written? Which is the smallest/largest amount of money?*

● *Which coins would be best for paying £2.75? Why do you think that?*

Name	Date

Money

■ Work with a partner.

- ☐ Take turns to choose an amount of money between £1 and £5.
- ☐ Say it in pennies, for instance 256 pence.
- ☐ Each find a way of making that amount using the least number of coins that you can.
- ☐ Record the money in the chart.
- ☐ Do this nine more times.

Amount of money in pence	Amount of money in £.p	Coins chosen

Coins © The Royal Mint

Right angles

Key objective:
Identify right angles.

What you need
● A copy of the 'Right angles' assessment sheet for each child; a set of 2-D shape tiles for each group including shapes with four right angles, shapes with some right angles, and shapes with no right angles; an A3 enlargement of 'Right angles'; Blu-Tack.

Further support
Decide whether to ask an adult to work with the group and to ask the children to complete the work orally. Prepare a large sheet of paper with the three headings from the assessment sheet and ask the children to take turns to choose a shape, and decide where it belongs. Ask the child to point to each right angle. The shape can be placed on the sheet as a recording, and the children can sketch it onto their assessment sheet.

Oral and mental starter
Show the children a square shape tile and ask: *How many right angles does this have?* Ask the children to look around the classroom and find something with a right angle. Invite one child to take the square and 'prove' to the others by placing it against their chosen angle that they have found a right angle. Repeat this so that other children can have a turn.

Main assessment activity
Explain that you want to find out in this lesson how well the children can sort out shapes that have right angles. Provide each child with a copy of the 'Right angles' assessment sheet and give each group a set of 2-D shape tiles. Tell the children that they may find it useful to each take a shape tile to begin with. Read the sheet together and explain that you would like the children to sort the shapes by: has four right angles; has some right angles; has no right angles.

Ask the children to work individually to pick a shape, decide where it fits onto the sorting diagram, then to sketch their shape accurately. Explain that their sketches should be small so that other shapes will fit too. Challenge the more able children to sketch some more shapes with one, two or three right angles on the back of their sheet. Remind them if necessary that their shapes can have more than four sides.

Plenary
Review with the children how they sorted the shapes. Discuss each shape, how many right angles it has and where it fits onto the sorting diagram. Use the Blu-Tack to affix each shape to the A3 enlargement of 'Right angles'. Ask questions as the children respond to each shape, such as: *How can you tell that this is a right angle? How can you tell when a shape does not have a right angle?* And of the more able: *Which shapes did you find that have one/two/three right angles?* Invite the children to draw these onto the board for the others to check. Where appropriate, name the shape.

Name	Date

Right angles

- Sort the shapes that your teacher gives you.

- Find the shapes that have all right angles.

- Find the shapes that have some right angles.

- Find the shapes that have no right angles.

- Now record your findings by sketching the shapes onto this sorting diagram.

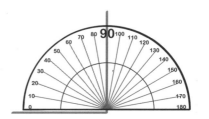

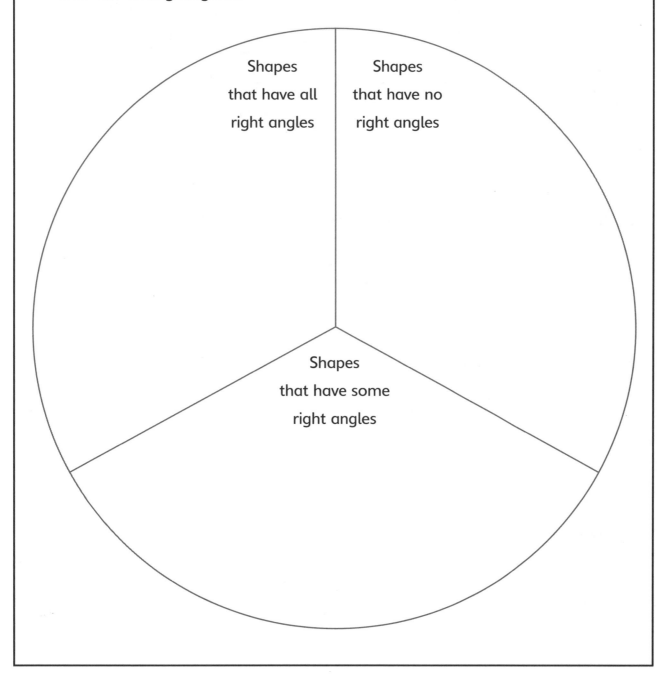

Shapes that have all right angles

Shapes that have no right angles

Shapes that have some right angles

Name   Date

Money and word problems

1. Money

Each amount of money has been written in pennies and in £.p.

Match the amounts that are worth the same by drawing a line between the pairs.

| 130p |
| 270p |
| 575p |
| 645p |

| £5.75 |
| £6.45 |
| £2.70 |
| £1.30 |

2. Word problems

◼ Jamie has £5 to spend. He buys two comics at £1.50 each.

How much do the comics cost? _____

How much change does he receive? _____

◼ Patti buys a CD for £4.25 and a chocolate bar for 50p.

How much does she spend? _____

How much change does she receive from £5? _____

◼ Bob buys a box of chocolates for his mum.

He gives the shopkeeper £5.

The shopkeeper gives Bob £2.30 in change.

How much does the box of chocolates cost? _____

Name	Date

Assessment 1

1. Write these numbers in words.

45	
98	
100	
134	
209	
560	

2. Write these numbers in numerals.

Sixty three	
Eighty nine	
One hundred and six	
Three hundred and forty eight	
Nine hundred and nine	
Nine hundred and ninety	

3. Write these numbers as hundreds + tens + units. The first one is done for you.

	Hundreds	Tens	Units
123	100	20	3
351			
602			
950			
517			

Name   Date

4. Circle each right angle in these shapes.

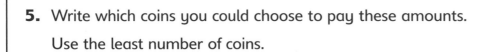

5. Write which coins you could choose to pay these amounts.
Use the least number of coins.

80p	
£1.50	
£2.25	
£5.65	
£6.08	
£4.99	

6. Write the answers to these word problems.

◖ Marisa bought five oranges at 30p each.

How much did the oranges cost? _____

How much change did she receive from £2? _____

◖ Peter paid £2.50 for a book and £1.30 for a pencil case.

How much did he pay in total? _____

What was his change from £5? _____

Assess and Review

Key objectives to be assessed

Assessment lesson 1: **Count on or back in tens or hundreds from any two- or three-digit number.**

Assessment lesson 2: **Recognise unit fractions such as 1/2, 1/3, 1/4, 1/5, 1/10, and use them to find fractions of shapes and numbers.**

Photocopiable pages
Guess the number (p95); Fraction count (p97); Fractions, word problems and Carroll diagrams (p98); Assessment test (p99-100).

Equipment
Teacher's and pupils' sets of 0–9 numeral cards; cubes.

Assessment Activities

Mental maths assessment

1. Counting
Ask the children to count on and back in tens. Begin counting from any number such as 20 or 42 for at least twenty counts, then back again. Repeat this for counting in hundreds from any three-digit number such as counting back from 720 to 120 and back again.

Probing questions
● *If you count in tens from 31, which digit changes? Why does the units digit stay the same?*
● *If you count in hundreds from 245, which digit changes? Why does the tens/units digit stay the same?*

2. Time Passing h
Explain that you will ask questions about time. Ask the children to put up their hands to answer. Ask, for example: *How many days are there in the week? How many days/weeks/months are there in the year? What is the date today? What will it be tomorrow?*

Probing questions
● *When is your birthday? How far away is that?*
● *What units of time will you use to answer that question?*
● *How long have you lived in your house? What units of time did you choose? Why are these good units to choose to answer this question?*

Written maths assessment

Provide copies of the assessment sheet 'Fractions, word problems and Carroll diagrams'. Either ask all the children in the class to complete this sheet and then ask the probing questions listed below of a group you wish to assess, or work with a targeted group and use the probing questions as the children work. Check that the children understand what to do for each part of the sheet.

Probing questions
As they work, ask of individuals:
c
● *Which would you rather have, 1/3 of £30 or 1/4 of £60? Why?*
● *Of which shapes is it easy to find 1/2, 1/4, 1/3, 1/5, 1/10? Why?*
● *Of which numbers is it easy to find 1/2, 1/4, 1/3, 1/5, 1/10? Why?*

j
● *How did you know that you needed to add/subtract/multiply/divide to find the answer?*
● *What clues were there in the problem?*
● *Make up a word problem that can be solved by calculating 36 + 19.*
● *What are the important things to remember when solving word problems?*

● *Show me a way to sort these numbers onto a Carroll diagram. What heading would you write onto the diagram?*
● *Can you show me another way to do this?*

Guess the number

Key objective:
Count on or back in tens or hundreds from any two- or three-digit number.

What you need
● Two sets of 0–9 numeral cards for each pair; two teaching sets of 0–9 numeral cards; a copy of the assessment sheet 'Guess the number' for each child.

Further support
Decide whether to limit the less able children to counting in tens only, using two-digit numbers. If the children are unsure, begin with counts forward. If they still find this difficult provide a 100-square so that they can use this to help them to count in tens.

Oral and mental starter
Count together, in tens, from 56 to 356 and back again. Ask: *If we count four tens from 59 what number do we reach? If we count back in tens from 543, how many tens do we need to count to reach 493?* Repeat this for counting in hundreds, forward and backwards, such as counting in hundreds from 234 or starting at 986 and counting back for five hundreds and predicting the number that will be reached.

Main assessment activity
Shuffle the teaching set of numeral cards and then invite a child to take the top two cards and to make a two-digit number. So, for example, for the cards 4 and 5 they could make 45 or 54. Now ask the children to think about what number would be reached if they counted five tens. From 45 they would count: *55, 65, 75, 85, 95.* Repeat this for another two-digit starting number. Now ask a child to take the top three cards from the stack and to make a three-digit number. This time there will be six possible numbers. For example, for cards 1, 2 and 3 the possibilities are: 123, 132, 213, 231, 312 and 321. Repeat the activity, this time asking the children to decide what number they would reach if they counted four, five or six hundreds forwards or backwards.

Explain that you would like the children to work in pairs with two sets of 0–9 numeral cards and a copy each of the assessment sheet 'Guess the number'. They should take turns to choose two numeral cards from the stack and make a two-digit number. The partner of the child who makes the number decides whether the other child should count on or back in tens, and how many tens. The child who counts makes a prediction of the final number, writes it on the sheet, then counts and writes the number that they reach. They should take five turns each at this, then repeat the activity for counting in hundreds.

Plenary
Ask the children to explain how they predicted the number that they would reach. Now ask them to repeat the activity, counting together, forwards or backwards, for two-digit numbers, then three-digit numbers. Ask probing questions such as:
● *What do you look for when finding a number 10 less/10 more than a given number?*
● *What do you look for when finding a number 100 less/100 more than a given number?*
● *Which digit always stays the same when counting in tens? Why is that?*
● *Which digit always stays the same when counting in hundreds? Why is that?*

WEEK 14 LESSON 1 ▭ End-of-term assessment

Name   Date

Guess the number

◪ Work with a partner.

☐ You will need two sets of 0–9 numeral cards.

☐ Take turns to take the top two cards from the stack.

☐ Make a two-digit number and write it on the chart.

☐ Tell your partner the number.

☐ Your partner decides how many tens you should count, and whether you should count forwards or backwards. Record this on the chart.

☐ Guess what number you will reach and write this on the chart.

☐ Count to see what number you reach and write this on the chart.

☐ Now swap over.

☐ Have four more turns each.

The number	How many tens forwards or backwards?	I guess that I will reach this number	The number I reach

◪ Now do this again. This time choose three cards and make an HTU number.

The number	How many hundreds forwards or backwards?	I guess that I will reach this number	The number I reach

PHOTOCOPIABLE

Fraction count

Key objective:
Recognise unit fractions such as 1/2, 1/3, 1/4, 1/5, 1/10, and use them to find fractions of shapes and numbers.

What you need
● 24 cubes for each pair; a copy of the assessment sheet 'Fraction count' for each child.

Further support
Decide whether to ask children who are less confident to work with a smaller quantity of cubes, such as 10 or 12. Encourage them to explain how to find 1/2, 1/4 of a quantity. Check that they understand that, for example, it is not possible to find exactly 1/3 of 10, nor is it possible to find exactly 1/5 of 12.

Oral and mental starter
Explain that you will ask the children to find half of the numbers that you say and to write the answer onto their whiteboards. When you say 'Show me', they should hold up their whiteboards. Say, for example: *What is half of 10... 16... 20... 40... 80... 100... 400... 800... 900.* Keep the pace sharp. Observe which children answer with ease, and which children need more experience of finding halves.

Main assessment activity
Ask a child to count out 12 cubes. Invite the children to say what half of the cubes would be, and then to separate the cubes into two equal piles and count each pile. Agree that half of 12 is 6. Repeat this for another fraction, such as finding a quarter.

Explain to the children that you would like them to work in pairs. They should count out 24 cubes and find 1/2, 1/4, 1/3 of these, then check to see if they could find 1/5 and 1/10 of 24. Ask them to write a sentence to explain their findings. Then, using 20 cubes, ask the children to find 1/2, 1/4, 1/5 and 1/10 of these and check to see if it is possible to find 1/3 of 20. Once again, ask them to write a sentence to explain what they find.

Plenary
Invite the children to explain how to find 1/2, 1/4 and 1/3 of 24. Discuss how they decided to do this. Some may have placed the cubes into equal groups, for example, finding two, four or three equal groups. The more able children may have used their knowledge of times-table facts to find the solution. Discuss each method.

Ask questions such as: *Can you find exactly 1/5 of 24? Why not?* Encourage the children to explain their thinking. Repeat this for 1/10 of 24 and 1/3 of 20. Ask: *Which numbers are easy to find 1/2 of? Why is this? What about 1/3... 1/4... 1/5... 1/10? What is special about the numbers that you choose?* Challenge the more able children to say another number where it is easy to find 1/2, 1/4 and 1/5 (40, for example).

Name   Date

Fraction count

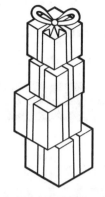

■ Work with a partner.

  ❑ You will need 24 cubes.

  ❑ Decide how to find $\frac{1}{2}$ of the cubes.

  ❑ Write the answer in the table.

  ❑ Do this again for $\frac{1}{3}$ and $\frac{1}{4}$.

$\frac{1}{2}$ of 24	$\frac{1}{3}$ of 24	$\frac{1}{4}$ of 24

■ Now think about the fractions $\frac{1}{5}$ and $\frac{1}{10}$.

  ❑ Is it possible to find $\frac{1}{5}$ of the cubes?

  ❑ What about $\frac{1}{10}$?

  ❑ Write a sentence about this.

I found out _____

■ Now try again for 20 cubes.

  ❑ Can you find: $\frac{1}{2}$? $\frac{1}{4}$? $\frac{1}{5}$? $\frac{1}{10}$?

  ❑ Fill in the chart.

$\frac{1}{2}$ of 20	$\frac{1}{4}$ of 20	$\frac{1}{5}$ of 20	$\frac{1}{10}$ of 20

■ What about $\frac{1}{3}$ of 20?

  ❑ Write a sentence about this.

I found out _____

Name   Date

Fractions, word problems and Carroll diagrams

1. Fractions

Look at the sets. Write how many there are in the fraction.

Total number of children in group	Number of boys	Fraction
24	12	
16	4	
18	6	
20	4	
30	3	

2. Word problems

Write the answer to these word problems.

The headteacher buys five packets of pencils. Each packet of pencils has eight pencils inside. How many pencils are there altogether?

_____

The headteacher gives Class 3 all the packets of pencils. There are 29 children and each child is given a new pencil. How many new pencils are left?

_____

Dan and Sam sharpen half of the new pencils. How many pencils do they sharpen?

_____

3. Carroll diagrams

Use the numbers from 20 to 50.

Find all the numbers that are a multiple of 5.

Now sort the numbers onto the Carroll diagram.

Write the headings on the diagram.

Now use the same numbers.

Find a different way to sort them.

Write the headings onto a new Carroll diagram.

Write in the numbers.

Name   Date

Assessment 2

1. Write the missing numbers.

25	35	45	55				

256	246	236	226				

143	243	343					843

907	807					307	207

2. Write the answers to these questions about time.

How many days are there in a week? _____

How many days are there in a year? _____

How many weeks are there in a year? _____

How many months are there in a year? _____

Write the date for your birthday _____

3. Write the fraction of the shaded part of each shape.

 Ⓐ

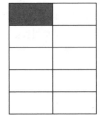 Ⓑ

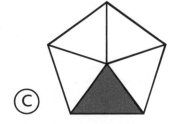 Ⓒ

 Ⓓ

AUTUMN ASSESSMENT

Name _____ Date _____

4. You have £5 to spend at the shop. Which three things will you buy? Find the total and work out your change. There is room for you to write jottings to help you.

BOSH! 85p
Paddy £2.20
70p
65p
STICKERS £1.25
£1.30

Choose three different things and find the total and the change.

I bought _____ , _____

and _____

The total is _____

My change from £5 is _____

5. The children in Class 3 collected data about their favourite flavours of crisps. Each child had one vote and everybody in the class voted.

a. Which was the most popular flavour of crisps?

_____

b. How many children are there in Class 3?

_____

c. Which flavour of crisps was the least popular?

_____

d. How many fewer children liked smoky bacon than ready salted crisps?

_____

Crisps	Favourite flavour
Ready salted	8
Salt and vinegar	5
Cheese and onion	6
Lamb & mint sauce	4
Chicken tikka	3
Chilli	1
Smoky bacon	4
Paprika	2

e. Which two flavours of crisps had the same number of votes?

_____ and _____

f. If you did this survey in your class, would you get the same results?

_____

g. Explain why you think this _____

Assess and Review

Key objectives to be assessed

Assessment lesson 1: **Know by heart facts for the 2, 5 and 10 multiplication tables.**
Assessment lesson 2: **Choose and use appropriate operations (including multiplication and division) to solve word problems, explaining methods and reasoning.**

Photocopiable pages

Cover it (p103); School time (p105); At the park (p106); Assessment test (p107-108).

Equipment

Individual whiteboards and pens; counters; blue and red felt-tipped pens.

Assessment Activities

Mental maths assessment

Multiplication facts f

Explain that you will ask the children multiplication facts for the 2, 5 and 10 times-tables. You may wish to deal with each table separately at first, to check that the children do know all the facts for these tables. Repeat the assessment, asking mixed questions from all three multiplication tables. Children can respond by writing the answers onto their whiteboards and, when you say 'Show me', by holding up the board for you to check.

Probing questions

● Write down □ x 5 = 30 and ask: *What is the missing number?* Repeat for other table facts and missing numbers.
● Write down □ x △ = 20. Ask: *What could the missing numbers be?*

Written maths assessment

Provide copies of the assessment sheet 'At the park'. Either ask all the children in the class to complete this sheet and then ask the probing questions listed below of a group you wish to assess, or work with a targeted group and use the probing questions as the children work. Check that the children understand what to do for each part of the sheet.

Probing questions j

As they work, ask of individuals:
● *How did you know which operation to choose?*
● *Make up a word problem using this calculation: 45 ÷ 5 = 9.*
● *What are the important things to remember when solving problems?*

Cover it

Key objective:
Know by heart facts for the 2, 5 and 10 multiplication tables.

What you need
● A copy of the 'Cover it' assessment sheet for each pair of children; 15 counters for each child (15 red and 15 blue for each pair); A3 enlargement of 'Cover it'; blue and red felt-tipped pens.

Further support
There may be some children for whom it would be more appropriate to concentrate on just the 2 times-table. Ask an adult to work with these children. The adult can write the 'answers' for the 2 times-table onto the flipchart: 2, 4, 6 and so on. The adult begins by pointing to one of the children and to a number from the board. If the child gives the correct answer they choose a number from the board for the next child to say the multiplication sentence. This can be repeated for the 5 and 10 times-tables, as appropriate.

Oral and mental starter
Explain that you will say the 'answer' to a multiplication by 2, 5 or 10, such as 20. Ask the children to suggest what the 'question' was. For 20, this could be 2 x 10, 10 x 2, 5 x 4 or 4 x 5. Keep the pace of this sharp. Use 'answers' such as 30, 40 and 15. If preferred, concentrate on one set of table facts, such as the 'answers' to the 2 times-table, then 5s, then 10s.

Main assessment activity
Pin the A3 enlargement of 'Cover it' onto the board. Explain the game to the children: *This is a game for two people. Take turns to choose a number from the grid and a multiplication table number of 2, 5 or 10.* Now demonstrate what happens if the 2 is chosen with 18 from the grid: *We can make a multiplication fact with 2 and 18 like this: something multiplied by 2 makes 18. What is the missing number?* Agree that the missing number is 9. Explain that if their partner agrees that their number sentence is correct then the child should cover their number on the grid.

Encourage the children to begin playing the game in pairs. They will need a copy of 'Cover it' and 15 counters in red for one player and blue for the other. As the children work at the game, listen in to the conversations of the children you wish to assess; that is, those for whom you are not yet sure that they know the table facts for 2, 5 and 10 times-tables.

Plenary
Using the A3 enlargement of 'Cover it', ask the children to play the game as a class. Divide the class into two teams, and appoint a captain for each team. Give one captain a red pen and the other one a blue pen. Ask the captains to take turns to choose a number from the grid. The captain of the other teams chooses one of the team members to state a multiplication fact with that number as the answer. The captain of the team with the correct answer can cross the number off the grid. The winning team is the one with more numbers crossed out on the grid.

Ask probing questions of the children who answer the questions, such as:
● *How did you work that out?*
● *If I said '20', what multiplication sentences can you say with 20 as the answer?*

Name   Date

Cover it

■ Play this game with a friend.

☐ You will each need some counters.

☐ Take turns to choose 2, 5 or 10 and a number from the grid.

☐ Now say the multiplication fact that you can make with your two numbers. For instance, if you choose 2 and 18 you can say 9 to make 9 x 2 = 18.

☐ If your partner agrees with your multiplication fact, cover the number that you chose on the grid with your counter.

☐ Repeat this until all the numbers are covered.

☐ The winner is the player with most counters on the grid.

2	5	10

50	6	18	45	12	70
2	10	35	15	90	8
25	100	4	60	16	40
30	5	80	20	55	14

School time

Key objective:
Choose and use appropriate operations (including multiplication and division) to solve word problems, explaining methods and reasoning.

What you need
● A copy of the assessment sheet 'School time' for each child.

Further support
Ask an adult to work with the less able children. The adult should read each question aloud with the children, then ask questions such as: *What information do we need in this question? What sort of operation do we need to do?* Then the children can work out the answer. An adult should ask the children how they calculated the answer.

Oral and mental starter

Explain that you will ask an addition question. Invite the children to give the answer and to explain how they worked this out. Begin with the addition of a decade number to a TU number, such as 40 + 35. Keep the pace sharp. Extend to adding near doubles such as 17 + 19.

Main assessment activity

Explain that you will read a short story and that each time you pause you would like the children to find the answer to the question. Say: *Fifty children take school lunches and 39 children bring sandwiches. How many children eat at school each lunch-time?* (89.) *If 14 children go home for lunch, how many children are there altogether at the school?* (103.) *The children have half an hour to eat their lunch each day. Then they can play outside for 20 minutes. How long is the lunch break?* (50 minutes.) *How many minutes does lunch break take up for the whole school week?* (5 x 50 minutes = 250 minutes.)

Now explain that you would like the children to work individually to solve the word problems on the assessment sheet 'School time'. As the children work, target a group of children whose ability to solve word problems you need to assess. Ask questions such as: *How did you know that you needed to add/ subtract/multiply/divide to find the solution?*

Plenary

Review the questions on the assessment sheet 'School time' together. Target individual children whose ability to solve word problems you need to assess and ask them to explain how they worked out the answer. Ask questions such as:
● *What do we need to find out?*
● *Which number operation do we need to use?*
● *Why do you think that? Which word(s) tell you that?*
Ask the children to explain which questions they tackled mentally, and which ones they needed to make jottings.

| Name | Date |

School time

◼ Read the questions carefully. Write your jottings. Write your answers.

1. There are 29 children in Class 3A, 35 children in class 3B and 30 children in class 3C. How many children are there altogether in Year 3?

2. In Year 2 there are 87 children altogether.

How many more children are there in Year 3 than in Year 2?

3. Mrs Jones is the teacher for Class 3C.

She decides to give each child in her class two new pencils. How many pencils will she need?

4. Mr Bryant is the teacher for class 3B.

He wants to seat his children in groups of five. How many groups of five can he make?

SPRING ASSESSMENT

Name	Date

At the park

◀ Read these questions about the park. Write your jottings on this sheet. Write your answers.

1. James and Robert go to the park every day after school.

They arrive at 4.30 and leave at 5 o'clock. How much time do they spend at the park during a school week?

2. The ice-cream van comes to the park every day.

The children buy ten ice lollies at 40p each and half that amount of ice-cream cones at 50p each. How much money do the children spend at the van each day?

3. The path from the beginning of the park to the play area is four times as long as the climbing frame. The climbing frame is three metres long. How long is the path?

4. On Monday 30 children use the play park.

On Tuesday half as many children use the park.

During the rest of the week 46 children use the park.

How many children in total use the park that week?

Name	Date

Assessment 3

1. Write the answers to these multiplication sentences.

5 x 2 = ☐	3 x 10 = ☐
6 x 5 = ☐	7 x 2 = ☐
10 x 10 = ☐	6 x 10 = ☐
8 x 5 = ☐	7 x 2 = ☐
9 x 2 = ☐	6 x 10 = ☐
7 x 5 = ☐	4 x 5 = ☐

2. Write in the missing numbers.

8 x ◯ = 16	◯ x 10 = 90
◯ x 5 = 40	7 x ◯ = 35
◯ x 10 = 50	9 x ◯ = 18
◯ x 2 = 8	◯ x 10 = 80
3 x ◯ = 15	◯ x 5 = 45

WEEK 7 ◻ Half-term assessment

Name _____ Date _____

3. Write in the missing numbers.

Make each number sentence different.

◯ x ☐ = 20	◯ x ☐ = 20
◯ x ☐ = 20	◯ x ☐ = 20

4. Read these word problems carefully. Write your jottings and your answers.

Questions	Jottings	Answer
Sum Mai bought three packets of sweets. Each packet had ten sweets in it. How many sweets did she buy?		
Sum Mai gave half of her sweets to her brother. How many did she have left?		
Sum Mai worked out that she had paid 10p for each sweet. How much did she spend on sweets altogether?		
Sum Mai counted how much money she had. Her father gave her £2, her mother gave her £1.75 and her uncle gave her £1.50. How much money did she have altogether?		

www.scholastic.co.uk

Assess and Review

Key objectives to be assessed
Assessment lesson 1: **Understand division and recognise that division is the inverse of multiplication.**
Assessment lesson 2: **Solve a given problem by organising and interpreting numerical data in simple lists, tables and graphs.**

Photocopiable pages
Division hop (p111); Favourite fruits (p113); Number sort (p114); Assessment test (p115-116).

Equipment
Individual whiteboards and pens; red and blue counters; number lines.

Assessment Activities

Mental maths assessment
Division facts g
Explain that you will ask some division questions. Ask the children to write the answers onto their whiteboards. When you say 'Show me', the children should hold up their boards for you to see their answers. Ask questions such as: *What is 20 divided by 2? How many 5s are there in 40? If I shared 30 sweets between five children, how many would each receive? What is 11 divided by 1?* Continue with similar questions, using multiplication table facts that the children know so that they can derive the division facts.

Probing questions
● *Tell me some numbers that will divide exactly by 2... by 5... by 10.*
● *If I divide a number by 5, then multiply the answer by 5, what happens?*
● *Is 4 ÷ 2 the same as 2 ÷ 4? Why not?*

Written maths assessment
Provide copies of the assessment sheet 'Number sort'. Either ask all the children in the class to complete this sheet and then ask the probing questions listed below of a group you wish to assess, or work with a targeted group and use the probing questions as the children work. Check that the children understand what to do for each part of the sheet.

Probing questions m
As they work, ask of individuals:
● *Which numbers do not go into the circle?* (Odd numbers.)
● *What is special about the numbers inside the circle?* (They are all even.)
● *If you continued beyond 100, what would the next number be to go inside the circle... and the next?*

Division hop

Key objective:
Understand division and recognise that division is the inverse of multiplication.

What you need
● A copy of the assessment sheet 'Division hop' for each pair of children; about 15 red and 15 blue counters for each pair; number lines; an A3 enlargement of 'Division hop'.

Further support
Some children may find it helpful to have a number line handy so that they can use this to make equal hops for division. If possible, ask an adult to work with this group and to play the game as a group. They should discuss each question and discover how the child found the answer.

Oral and mental starter
Explain that you will say a division fact. Invite the children to put up their hands to say the answer. Then ask them to find a multiplication fact that uses the same numbers. So, for example, for $16 \div 2 = 8$, the children would find $8 \times 2 = 16$. Repeat this for other division facts from the 2, 5 and 10 times-tables.

Main assessment activity
Explain that you would like the children to play a game in pairs. Pin up the A3 copy of 'Division hop' and explain that the children will take turns to choose a square on the grid and answer the question. If their partner agrees with the answer, they can place a counter over that square. When all the squares are covered, the winner is the one with most counters on the grid.

Ask the children to begin the game and to play one round each. Now stop and check that everyone understands what to do. As the children play the game, target those children for whom you need further assessment information about their ability with division. Ask questions such as: *How did you work out the answer? Can you tell me a multiplication that uses those numbers? Is $14 \div 2$ the same as $2 \div 14$? Why not?*

Where children do not yet know the table facts for the grid questions, provide a number line so that they can make equal hops along it to find the solution. At this stage it is the understanding of what is meant by division that is most important. However, note any children who need a number line as these children would benefit from further work on learning multiplication tables.

Plenary
Discuss the strategies that the children used to find the solutions to the grid questions. Where children used number lines, ask: *How can multiplication tables help us with division?* Elicit that if a multiplication fact is known then the linked division fact can easily be found, such as $4 \times 3 = 12$ and $12 \div 3 = 4$. Choose some of the questions and ask probing questions such as:
● *How can you tell if 27 is a multiple of 3?*
● *So why is 26 not a multiple of 3?*
● *Is $16 \div 2$ the same as $2 \div 16$? Why not?*
● *If $81 \div 9$ is 9, what would 9×9 be?*
● *If 8×6 is 54, what would $54 \div 6$ be?*
● *What is $12 \div 1$?*

Division hop

■ Play this game with a friend.

☐ You will each need some coloured counters.

☐ Take turns to choose a question from the grid.

☐ Say the answer.

☐ If your partner agrees with your answer, cover the question with one of your counters.

☐ The winner is the player with more counters on the grid at the end of the game.

$15 \div 3$	$20 \div \boxed{} = 4$	$70 \div 10$	Is 27 a multiple of 3?
$50 \div 10$	How many 5p coins do you get for 35p?	How many 5m lengths are there in a 45m rope?	Is 26 a multiple of 3?
Half of 20?	Is 40 a multiple of 5?	How many plates of 5 cakes can you get from 40 cakes?	Divide 30 by 5
$18 \div 3$	$24 \div 4$	$60 \div 10$	Divide 18 by 2
$24 \div 3$	$30 \div 5$	$21 \div 3$	$40 \div 10$

Favourite fruits

Key objective:
Solve a given problem by organising and interpreting numerical data in simple lists, tables and graphs.

What you need
● Paper; a copy of the assessment sheet 'Favourite fruits' for each child; an A3 enlargement of 'Favourite fruits'.

Further support
Decide whether to use an A3 enlargement of the assessment sheet 'Favourite fruits', pinned to a flipchart, and ask an adult to work with the less able children as a group. They carry out the task as a group, taking turns to write onto the sheet. The adult should ask questions as the children work, such as: *How many children liked strawberries best? So where do we draw the bar for the strawberries?*

Oral and mental starter

Ask the children to help you to sort some numbers onto a Venn diagram. Draw this diagram:

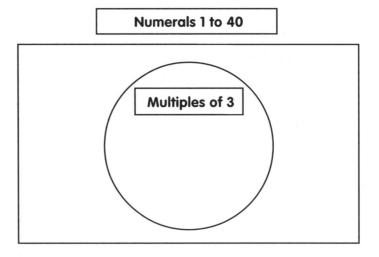

Invite the children to suggest where each numeral from 1 to 40 fits on the diagram. Repeat this for another Venn diagram labelled 'Multiples of 10' using the number range 100 to 300.

Main assessment activity

Explain that in this assessment lesson you would like to find out how well the children can collect data, put it into a frequency table, and make a bar chart from it. Begin by giving the children time to collect the data. Ask them to work in groups of eight to collect data about their favourite fruits. Write a list of fruits onto the board: bananas, oranges, apples, pears, strawberries, grapes and cherries, from which the children each choose their favourite. This will limit the range of data that they collect to a manageable set. Provide each child with a sheet of paper and ask them to collect the data onto the sheet, deciding how they will do this for their group. In this way, each child will collect and organise the data. When the groups have collected their data, invite each group to write it on the board, onto a class frequency table. Now provide each child with assessment sheet 'Favourite fruits' and ask them to organise the information onto the bar chart. As the children work at this task individually, take time to talk to the children whose data handling skills you are wish to assess.

Plenary

Pin an A3 enlargement of 'Favourite fruits' to the board. Invite the children that you are targeting to come to the board and draw a bar for the fruit that you say, until the chart is complete. Now ask probing questions such as:
● *How many more children liked _____ than _____?*
● *How can you tell this?*
● *Which is the least popular fruit?*
● *Tell me a sentence about the most and least popular fruits.*
● *Most children in this class like cherries best. How could we find out if this is true?*

Name   Date

 **Favourite fruits**

◀ Use the information that your class collected about favourite fruits.

◀ Make a bar chart.

Number of children		Bananas	Oranges	Apples	Pears	Straw-berries	Grapes	Cherries
11								
10								
9								
8								
7								
6								
5								
4								
3								
2								
1								

Fruit

◀ Answer these questions about your data.

1. Which is the most popular fruit? _____

2. Which is the least popular fruit? _____

3. How many children voted? _____

Name   Date

Number sort

◼ Sort the set of numbers 50 to 100 onto the Venn diagram.

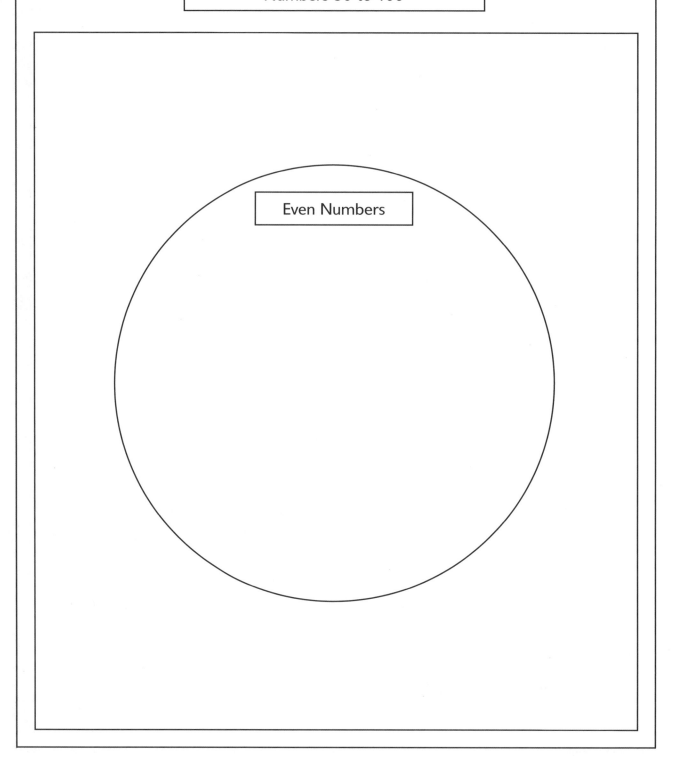

Numbers 50 to 100

Even Numbers

Name   Date

Assessment 4

1. Write the answer to the multiplication sentence.
Write a division sentence which matches the multiplication
sentence. The first one is done for you.

10 x 3 = $\boxed{30}$	$\boxed{30}$ ÷ $\bigcirc\!\!\!\!10$ = $\diagbox{3}$
4 x 2 = ☐	☐ ÷ ○ = ▱
5 x 5 = ☐	☐ ÷ ○ = ▱
6 x 10 = ☐	☐ ÷ ○ = ▱
9 x 2 = ☐	☐ ÷ ○ = ▱
10 x 10 = ☐	☐ ÷ ○ = ▱
7 x 5 = ☐	☐ ÷ ○ = ▱
6 x 3 = ☐	☐ ÷ ○ = ▱
9 x 3 = ☐	☐ ÷ ○ = ▱
4 x 3 = ☐	☐ ÷ ○ = ▱
10 x 2 = ☐	☐ ÷ ○ = ▱

SPRING ASSESSMENT

Name   Date

2. Write the answers to these questions.

a. Share 16 between 2.

b. Find half of 40.

c. What do I divide by 2 to get 6?

d. The supermarket packs biscuits in tens.
    How many packs can be made from 90 biscuits?

3. Sort the numbers 1 to 30 onto this Venn Diagram.

Numbers 1 to 30

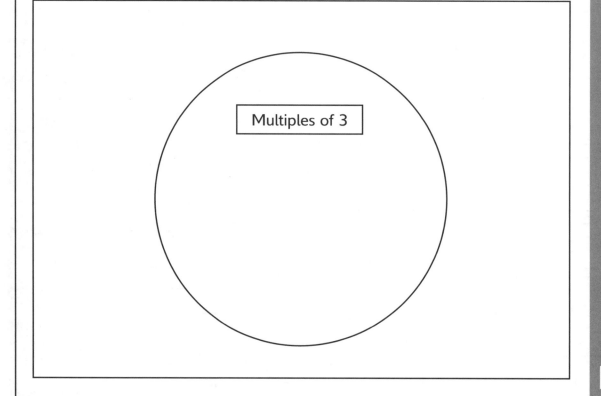

Multiples of 3

Assess and Review

Key objectives to be assessed

Assessment lesson 1: **Read, write and order whole numbers to at least 1000; know what each digit represents.**

Assessment lesson 2: **Identify lines of symmetry in simple shapes and recognise shapes with no lines of symmetry.**

Photocopiable pages
Make a number (p119); Alphabet search (p121); Challenges (p122); Assessment test (p123-124).

Equipment
Three teaching sets of 0-9 numeral cards; individual whiteboards and pens; pupil sets of 0-9 numeral cards; safety mirrors; sets of 2-D shape tiles.

Assessment Activities

Mental maths assessment

Hundreds, tens and units

Ask the children to draw this grid onto their whiteboards:

Hundreds	Tens	Units

Shuffle the three sets of teaching numeral cards and explain that you will hold up a numeral. Ask the children to write the numeral onto their grid. The aim is to make the largest number they can. Once the numeral is placed they cannot move it.

Probing questions
● *Did you always make the largest number possible?*
● *What is the largest number we could make with these three digits?*
● *What is the smallest number that we could make?*
● *What does the hundreds/tens/units digit represent?*

Written maths assessment

Provide copies of the assessment sheet 'Challenges'. Either ask all the children in the class to complete this sheet and then ask the probing questions listed below of a group you wish to assess, or work with a targeted group and use the probing questions as the children work. Check that the children understand what to do for each part of the sheet.

Probing questions
As they work, ask of individuals:

● *How did you add this near multiple of 10?*
● *Why is this a good method?*

● *How did you know you needed to add/subtract/multiply/divide?*
● *Make up a word problem that could be solved by multiplying 8 by 3.*

● *If this is half a symmetrical shape, how would you complete it to make a symmetrical shape?*
● *What do you look for when trying to find a line of symmetry in a shape?*

Make a number

Oral and mental starter

Explain that you would like each child in the class to write a three-digit number on their whiteboard. Ask them to make sure that their number is different from their nearest neighbour's. Give the children a moment to check this. Invite them to work in groups of four to place their numbers in order. Now invite two groups of four to come to the front of the class. Ask the other children to help to order the numbers. Ask probing questions such as:

● *Which is the lowest/highest number? How can you tell that?*
● *Which number comes next? How do you know that?*
● *In this number, what does the hundreds/tens/units digit represent?*

If there is time, invite other groups to come to the front and to slot their numbers into place until all the numbers are placed in order, from the lowest to highest. If any children have duplicate numbers, ask them to stand to one side and then to decide how to change their number so that they can join the number line.

Main assessment activity

Take three sets of numeral cards and shuffle them. Explain that you would like a child to take the top three cards, but not show anyone their cards. Invite another child to do the same. Now ask both children to make a three-digit number with their cards and to hold this up for the class to see. Ask: *Which is the larger number? How can you tell?*

Explain that you would like the children to work in pairs. The children take turns to take the top three cards from their shuffled stack of three sets of 0-9 cards. Then, without showing their partner, they make the largest number that they can with their cards and, when both are ready, place their cards on the table. The child who has the larger number wins that round. They can record their numbers, and who won that round, on the assessment sheet 'Make a number'. They continue to play for ten turns, then check to see who has won the game. If there is time, the children could play again, this time making the smallest possible number.

Plenary

Write a three-digit number onto the board, such as 819. Ask probing questions such as:

● *What does the 8/1/9 mean?*
● *What other numbers could I make with these three digits?*
● *Which is the largest/smallest number I could make with these digits?*
● *I have two numbers: 844 and 846. How can I tell which is larger?*

Name   Date

Make a number

◼ Work with a partner.

☐ You will need three sets of 0–9 numeral cards.

☐ Shuffle the cards.

☐ Take turns to take the top three cards.

☐ Do not show your partner the cards yet.

☐ Make the largest number you can.

☐ When you are both ready, put the cards down on the table.

☐ The one with the larger number wins that round.

☐ Write your numbers into the table.

☐ Play again nine more times.

Name	Number	Name	Number	Who won?

Alphabet search

Key objective:
Identify lines of symmetry in simple shapes and recognise shapes with no lines of symmetry.

What you need
● Safety mirrors; set of 2-D shape tiles for each group; a copy of the assessment sheet 'Alphabet search' for each child; an A3 enlargement of 'Alphabet search'.

Further support
Ask the less able children to work as a small group with an adult. Pin an A3 enlargement of 'Alphabet search' onto the flipchart. The children can check each letter on their own sheet, with a mirror, as well as taking turns to demonstrate with a mirror where the lines of symmetry are on the A3 sheet.

Oral and mental starter
Provide each group with a set of shape tiles. Explain that you will say a property of one of the shapes and would like the children to remove from their set those shapes that do not fit the property. You will repeat this until someone can work out which shape you are thinking of. Say, for example: *My shape has four sides. All its angles are right angles. It has four lines of symmetry.* The children should by now work out that this is a square. Repeat for other shapes, such as: *My shape has four sides. It has no right angles. It has no lines of symmetry.* (Quadrilateral)

Main assessment activity
Pin up the A3 version of 'Alphabet search'. Ask the children to look carefully at the letter A and ask: *Does this letter have any lines of symmetry?* Discuss with the children where the line of symmetry in the letter A is.

Provide each child with a copy of 'Alphabet search'. Ask the children to work individually to find which letters have one line of symmetry, and which have two. Explain that the children should draw in the lines of symmetry and complete the table on the sheet. Provide safety mirrors to help the children check for symmetry. As they work, focus upon those children whose understanding of symmetry you need to assess. Ask them to explain how they are checking each letter for lines of symmetry.

Plenary
Review the sheet together, using the A3 enlargement of 'Alphabet search'. Ask the children that you are targeting for assessment to take turns to draw in the lines of symmetry on individual letters. Ask probing questions such as:
● *How can you check that you have found all the lines of symmetry?*
● *Which letters do not have any lines of symmetry?*
● *What do you think the S would look like if we checked for symmetry with a mirror?*
● *What do you look for when trying to find a line of symmetry in a shape?*

Name   Date

Alphabet search

◀ Check each of these capital letters for lines of symmetry.

◀ Draw in the lines of symmetry that you find.

◀ Write the letters into the table.

Number of lines of symmetry		
0	1	2

A B C
D E F
G H I J
K L M
N O P
Q R S T
U V W
X Y Z

Name _____ Date _____

Challenges

1. Write the answers to these questions.

$29 + 34 =$	
$65 + 21 =$	
$273 - 9 =$	
$562 + 11 =$	
$73 - 49 =$	
$80 - 31 =$	

2. The farmer picks 40kg of apples.
How many 5kg sacks can he fill? _____

3. Sketch the lines of symmetry in these shapes.

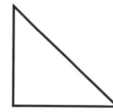

Name	Date

Assessment 5

1. Write these numbers in order, beginning with the smallest number.

132   695   402   461   555   199   796   679   976   697   967
769   305   999   799   654   350   156   465   405   436   497
466   406

_____

_____

_____

_____

2   Write the answers to these addition and subtraction sentences.

516 + 9 = ☐	85 – 19 = ☐
482 + 11 = ☐	45 – 21 = ☐
921 – 9 = ☐	54 + 39 = ☐
456 – 11 = ☐	65 – 39 = ☐
52 + 19 = ☐	51 + 41 = ☐
64 + 21 = ☐	60 – 41 = ☐

Name   Date

3. Write the answers to these word problems.

There is space for your jottings.

a. Eknath buys 45 red marbles and 29 green marbles.

How many marbles does he buy altogether? _____

b. Kunjal has 92 stickers that she has collected. She gives Rajiv

51 of her stickers. How many stickers has Kunjal now? _____

4. Make half a pattern on the left side of this paper.

☐ Now make the rest of the pattern, making sure that it is symmetrical.

☐ You can use a mirror to help you.

☐ You can colour your pattern, but make sure that your colouring keeps the pattern symmetrical.

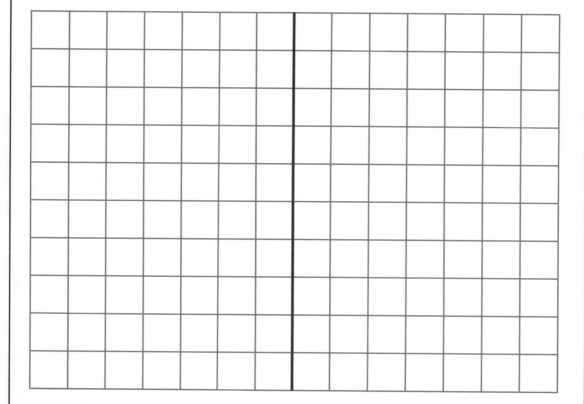

Assess and Review

Key objectives to be assessed
Assessment lesson 1: **Know by heart all addition and subtraction facts for each number to 20.**
Assessment lesson 2: **Add and subtract mentally a 'near multiple of 10' to or from a two-digit number.**

Photocopiable pages
Beat the clock (p127); Make a total (p129); Venn and Carroll diagrams (p130); Assessment test (p131-132).

Equipment
Individual whiteboards and pens; sets of 0–20 numeral cards; stop clocks or a clock with a second hand; counters; sets of 0–9 numeral cards.

Assessment Activities

Mental maths assessment

1. Addition and subtraction to 20 [d]
Explain that you will ask an addition or subtraction fact where the largest number will be 20 or less. Ask the children to write the answer on their whiteboards and, when you say 'Show me', to hold up their boards. Keep the pace sharp so that the children have about five seconds of thinking time as by now they should know these facts.

Probing questions
● *The answer is 14. Tell me what the addition question could be.*
● *The answer is 6. What could the subtraction question be?*

2. Near multiples of 10 [e]
Now invite the children to write the answer to the question that you say onto their whiteboards, then, when you say 'Show me', they hold their board up for you to see. Ask, for example: *What is 35 add 29? What is 46 add 41? What is 73 subtract 29? What is 87 subtract 51?*

Probing questions
● *How did you find the answer?*
● *Why is this a good method for adding 19? Or for subtracting 21?*

Written maths assessment
Provide copies of the assessment sheet 'Venn and Carroll diagrams'. Either ask all the children in the class to complete this sheet and then ask the probing questions listed below of a group you wish to assess, or work with a targeted group and use the probing questions listed below as the children work. Check that the children understand what to do for each part of the sheet.

Probing questions [m]
● *Which information goes into this part of the diagram?*
● *What label could you write for this diagram?*
● *How did you sort the numbers?*
● *Tell me another way to sort the numbers.*

☐ 125

Beat the clock

Key objective:
Know by heart all addition and subtraction facts for each number to 20.

What you need
● A set of 0-20 numeral cards for each pair; stop clocks or a clock with a second hand that everyone can see; a copy of the assessment sheet 'Beat the clock' for each pair; sheets of paper.

Further support
If the less able children are still unsure about number facts to 20 you may wish to assess how well they know their facts to 10 or 15. If this is the case then give a limited set of numeral cards for 0 to 10 or 15. Decide whether to allow this group to have longer, for example two minutes, in order to write down all the facts that they can find for each chosen number.

Oral and mental starter
Tell the children that in this lesson they will be working with addition and subtraction facts for numbers to 20. Explain that you will say an 'answer'. Ask the children to suggest what the question could be. Say, for example: *The answer is 17. What could the question be?* Write the children's answers onto the board, and then ask them to order the responses to make any pattern that they can see, such as: 1 + 16, 2 + 15, 3 + 14 or 20 – 3, 19 – 2, 18 – 1.

Main assessment activity
After shuffling a set of 0-20 numeral cards, ask a child to take the top card and show it to everyone. Now say: *All the addition sentences we are going to make today will include numbers up to, but not over, 20. Look at this number. What addition sentences can you make which include it?* Invite the children to make some suggestions and write these on the board. Now ask them to make subtraction sentences which include the chosen number and write those onto the board.

Explain to the children that you would like them to play a game with their partner. Say: *Take turns to choose a card. Agree when to start by looking at the clock. Give yourselves one minute and each of you, on a sheet of paper, write down all the addition and subtraction facts that you can think of that use that number. Remember, none of the numbers must be greater than 20. At the end of one minute count how many number facts you each have and write that on your sheet. The one with most number facts wins that round.*

Plenary
Explain that you will choose a number. Ask the children to take turns to give you a number fact. Write these under two headings, Add and Subtract, on the board. When the children have exhausted all the facts, ask: *How could we check that we have found all possible number facts? What patterns could we use?* Discuss how working systematically and ordering the facts will help them to find all the facts. Wipe the board and, choosing another number, repeat this – this time encouraging the children to suggest ways of ordering the facts so that they can find missing facts through the patterns that they can see.

Ask probing questions such as:
● *If I say 19, what sort of number sentences could I make?* ($\square$ + $\bigcirc$ = 19; $\bigcirc$ + $\square$ = 19; 19 – $\square$ = $\bigcirc$; 19 – $\bigcirc$ = $\square$).
● *What subtractions give an answer of 8?*
● *What additions give an answer of 17?*

Beat the clock

- Work with a partner.
  - ☐ You need a set of shuffled 0–20 cards and a sheet of paper each.
  - ☐ Take turns to take the top card and put it onto the table in front of both of you.
  - ☐ On a sheet of paper, write as many addition and subtraction sentences as you can using the number on the card. You have one minute to do this.
  - ☐ Check each other's number sentences and count how many there are.
  - ☐ Fill in the chart.
  - ☐ Repeat this until all the cards have been used up.
  - ☐ The winner is the player who won more rounds.

| | Name | Name | |
Number chosen	Number sentences	Number sentences	Who won?

Make a total

Key objective:
Add and subtract mentally a 'near multiple of 10' to or from a two-digit number.

What you need
● A copy of the assessment sheet 'Make a total'; a counter and two sets of 0-9 numeral cards for each pair.

Further support
Decide whether there are children in the class who would benefit from working with adding and subtracting just 9, 19, 11 and 21. They can carry out the activity in the same way if the assessment sheet spinner is adjusted. Encourage the children to explain how they calculated. If possible, get an adult to work with this group, and to ask about their calculation strategies.

Oral and mental starter

Explain that you will say a number sentence which includes a near multiple of 10. Ask the children to work mentally to find the answer. They can put their hands up to answer. Ask, for example: *What is 45 + 29? 36 + 21? 94 - 39? 84 - 51? How did you work out the answer?*

Main assessment activity

Get the children to work in pairs. Explain that you would like to find out how well they can work mentally to add and subtract near multiples of 10. Tell the children that you would like them to play a game. Give each pair a copy of 'Make a total', a counter and two sets of 0-9 numeral cards. Explain that they should take turns to toss the counter onto the spinner, then to take the top two numeral cards to make a TU number. The child then decides whether to add or subtract their spinner number to their card number so that the answer is less than 100. Their partner checks that the answer is right. Then the child who made the number sentence writes it into the chart on the sheet. At the end of ten turns each, the children check how many number sentences they calculated correctly and the winner is the one with more sentences correct.

As the children work, target children whose ability to mentally add and subtract near multiples of 10 you need to assess. Ask questions such as:
● *How did you work this out?*
● *Why is this a good method for adding/subtracting?*
● *What is the difference between adding 29 and subtracting 29 using this method?*

Plenary

Explain that you will say an addition or subtraction number sentence which uses near multiples of 10. Invite a child to say the answer. Say, for example: *What is 49 add 26? How did you work this out? So what is 76 subtract 49? How did you work that out? What do we need to do to add 29? Is this the same as subtracting 29?* Repeat this for other near multiples, such as 54 + 39, 87 - 39, 46 + 41, 76 - 41 and so on.

Name _____ Date _____

Make a total

■ Work with a partner.

☐ You will need a counter and two sets of shuffled 0–9 numeral cards.

☐ Now take turns to toss the counter onto the spinner on the sheet and to take the top two numeral cards.

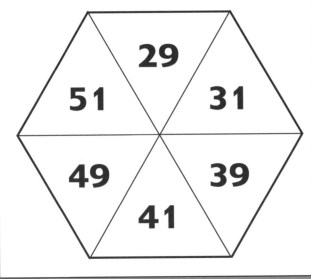

☐ Make a TU number with the cards and decide whether to add or subtract your card number and the spinner number.

☐ The answer must be less than 100.

☐ Write the number sentence into the chart.

☐ Ask your partner to check whether they agree with your answer.

☐ Do this ten times each.

☐ The player with more correct answers wins the game.

Number Spinner

29
51
31
49
39
41

Name _____	Name _____
Total of correct answers _____	Total of correct answers _____

SUMMER ASSESSMENT

Name   Date

Venn and Carroll diagrams

■ Decide how to sort the numbers 100 to 150 onto the Carroll diagram.

   ☐ Write labels.

   ☐ Write a title for your Carroll diagram.

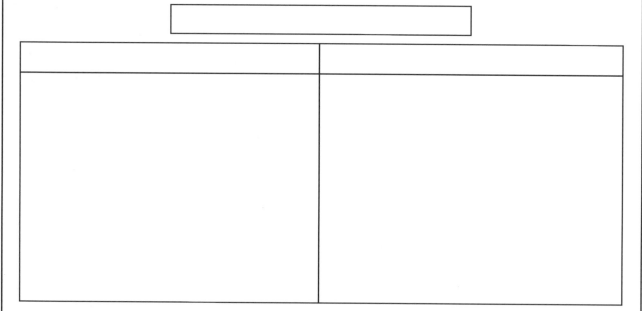

■ Now find another way to sort the numbers 100 to 150.

   ☐ Fill in this Venn diagram.

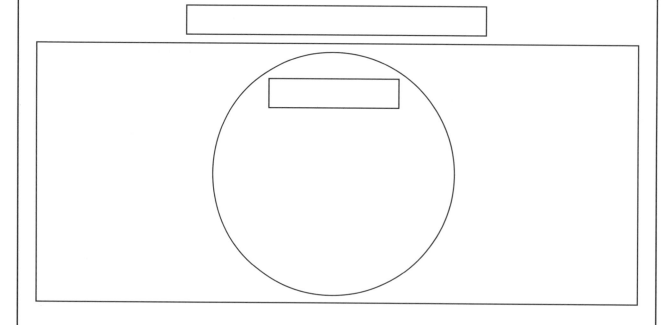

Name   Date

Assessment 6

1. Write the answers to these questions.

$14 + 5 = \boxed{}$	$\boxed{} + 12 = 19$
$19 - 16 = \boxed{}$	$4 + \boxed{} = 16$
$8 + 7 = \boxed{}$	$13 - \boxed{} = 6$
$20 - 13 = \boxed{}$	$\boxed{} - 8 = 15$
$15 + 5 = \boxed{}$	$18 - \boxed{} = 4$
$\boxed{} - 6 = 12$	$\boxed{} + 4 = 19$
$4 + \boxed{} = 13$	$16 + \boxed{} = 20$
$20 - \boxed{} = 20$	$\boxed{} - 13 = 6$
$5 + \boxed{} = 14$	$14 + \boxed{} = 15$
$\boxed{} + 6 = 14$	$\boxed{} + 3 = 19$

Name _____ Date _____

2. Check the answers to each of these number sentences.

Tick them if they are correct.

Put a cross if they are wrong and write the correct answer.

Number sentence	Right or wrong (✓ or ×)	Correct answer
25 + 19 = 44		
96 – 59 = 47		
54 + 29 = 75		
83 – 51 = 32		
17 + 59 = 86		
95 – 41 = 56		
83 – 59 = 13		
57 – 29 = 28		
46 + 39 = 87		
37 + 51 = 97		

3. The children in Class 3 collected information about where they would like to go on holiday.

This is what they collected.

Draw a bar chart to show this information.

Make the scale one rectangle for two children. Label your graph.

Holiday	Number of children
Alton Towers	8
Drayton Manor Park	6
Center Parcs	5
Chessington Zoo	7
Thorpe Park	3

End-of-year assessment

There are two forms of end-of-year assessment:
● Mental tests: there are two of these. Each has its own photocopiable sheet on which the children write their answers.
● Check-ups: these are written tests covering all the key objectives for the year.

The test questions are matched to the key objectives in the table below. Where you are still unsure whether a child has achieved a key objective, use the probing questions in the table for the relevant key objective to help you to make an informed decision about achievement.

Key objective	Mental test 1 question number	Mental test 2 question number	Written test question number	Probing questions
A	1, 2	1, 2	3, 4	*Use digit cards to show me the number 574. What does the 5/7/4 represent? Remove the 7. What number do you have now? What does the 5 represent now?*
B	3	3	7	*If you count back in tens from 67, why does the unit digit stay the same?*
C			5	*Which numbers is it easy to find a third/quarter/fifth/ tenth of? Why is that?*
D	4, 5, 6	4, 5, 6	1	*Tell me some subtractions that have the answer 7.*
E	13		6	*How do you add/subtract a near multiple of 10? Why is this a good method?*
F	7, 8, 9	7, 8, 9	1	*Which two numbers multiplied together make 24? Can you think of some more pairs of numbers which make a product of 24?*
G	10	10	2	*Is 6 divided by 2 the same as 2 divided by 6? Why not?*
H	11	11	8	*How long have you been a pupil at this school?*
I	12	12	9	*Order these amounts of money starting with the least: £0.17, 28p, £2.80, £1.17.*
J	13	13	9	*How did you know whether to add/subtract/multiply/ divide?*
K	14	14	10	*Sort these 2-D shapes into those with no right angles, one right angle, two/three/four right angles.*
L	15	15	11	*How can you tell if a shape is symmetrical?*
M	16	16	12	*How could you sort the numbers 20 to 50 onto a Venn diagram? A Carroll diagram? What criterion/criteria would you choose?*

Mental maths test 1

Instructions

Explain to the children that you will read each question twice.

Ask them to write their name and the date at the top of their recording sheet.

For questions 1 to 10, allow five seconds before moving on to the next question.

For questions 11 to 16, allow ten seconds.

Test 1

1. Write in numerals the number nine hundred and forty three.

2. For the number 832 write down the tens digit.

3. Count on five tens from 56. Write down the number that you reach.

4. What is 8 add 9?

5. What is the difference between 16 and 7?

6. How much more is 13 than 8?

7. What is 8 multiplied by 2?

8. What is 6 times 5?

9. What is the product of 7 and 10?

10. How many 5s are there in 40?

11. How many days are there in a fortnight?

12. I have £3 to spend. I buy a drink for 90p. How much money do I have now?

13. Peter buys 65 marbles. He buys another 21 marbles. How many does he have altogether?

14. Look at the quadrilateral on your sheet. Put a tick by its right angle.

15. Tick the shape that has no lines of symmetry.

16. Look at the graph. How many more apples were bought than pears?

| Name | | Date | |

Mental maths test I recording sheet

◤ Listen to the questions, then write your answers in the spaces provided.

◤ If you want to change an answer, cross out your first answer then write in the new one. Do not rub out.

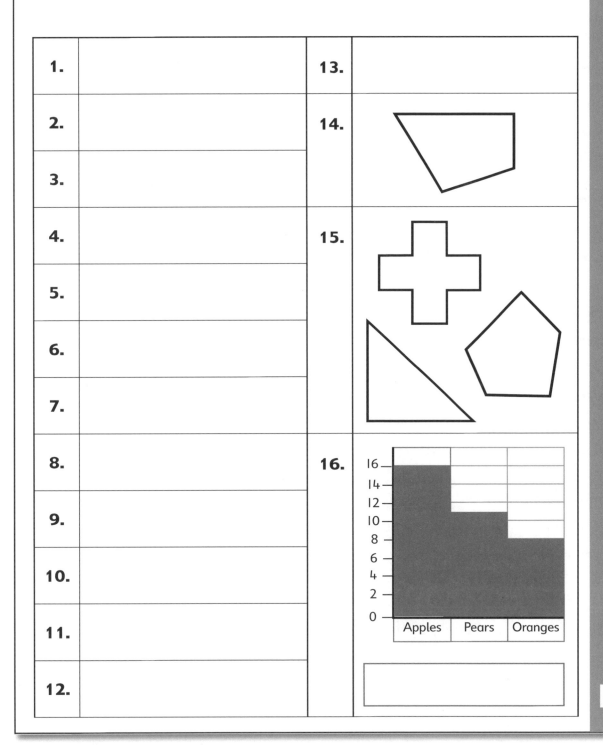

1.		13.	
2.		14.	
3.			
4.		15.	
5.			
6.			
7.			
8.		16.	
9.			
10.			
11.			
12.			

Mental maths test 2

Instructions

Explain to the children that you will read each question twice.

Ask them to write their name and the date at the top of their answer sheet.

For questions 1 to 10 allow 5 seconds before moving on to the next question.

For questions 11 to 16 allow 10 seconds.

Test 2

1. Write the number 406 in words.

2. Write down the hundreds digit for the number 840.

3. Count back three hundreds from 789.

4. What is the difference between 11 and 19?

5. How many fewer is 5 than 19?

6. What is the total of 8 and 11?

7. What is 5 multiplied by 10?

8. What is 4 times 2?

9. What is the product of 8 and 10?

10. What is 30 divided by 10?

11. I leave home at ten past eight. I get to school at 8.45. How long does it take me to get to school?

12. Kayleigh buys five comics at 80p each. How much does she spend?

13. There are 80 apples. Each box will hold 30 apples. How many boxes will be needed to hold the 80 apples?

14. Look at the shape on your sheet. Tick the right angle.

15. Look at the shape on your sheet. Draw in its two lines of symmetry.

16. Look at the graph. How many pets are there in total?

End-of-year assessment

Name		Date

Mental maths test 2 recording sheet

◾ Listen to the questions, then write your answers in the spaces provided.

◾ If you want to change an answer, cross out your first answer then write in the new one. Do not rub out.

1.		12.	
2.		13.	
3.		14.	
4.			
5.		15.	
6.			
7.			
8.		16.	
9.			
10			
11.			

📖 **End-of-year assessment**

Name	Date

Check-ups

1. Write the answers to these questions.

$9 + 8 = \boxed{}$	$7 \times 2 = \boxed{}$
$16 + 4 = \boxed{}$	$9 \times 5 = \boxed{}$
$17 - 9 = \boxed{}$	$10 \times 10 = \boxed{}$
$15 - 6 = \boxed{}$	$6 \times 2 = \boxed{}$
$13 - 6 = \boxed{}$	$7 \times 5 = \boxed{}$
$14 + 5 = \boxed{}$	$8 \times 10 = \boxed{}$
$14 - 6 = \boxed{}$	$8 \times 5 = \boxed{}$
$20 - 20 = \boxed{}$	$9 \times 2 = \boxed{}$
$13 - 9 = \boxed{}$	$4 \times 10 = \boxed{}$
$18 - 13 = \boxed{}$	$1 \times 2 = \boxed{}$

2. Use your multiplication tables to help you to find the answers to these division questions.

$15 \div 3 = \boxed{}$	$24 \div \boxed{} = 6$
$20 \div 5 = \boxed{}$	$35 \div \boxed{} = 5$
$30 \div 10 = \boxed{}$	$\boxed{} \div 4 = 8$

3. Write these numbers using numerals.

Five hundred and thirty five _____

Six hundred and seven _____

Four hundred and forty _____

Three hundred and twenty nine _____

End-of-year assessment

4. Write these numbers as hundreds, tens and units.
The first one is done for you.

	Hundreds	Tens	Units
Two hundred and thirty six	200	30	6
One hundred and nineteen			
Three hundred and twenty			
Four hundred and eight			
Six hundred and ninety nine			

5. Find the fractions of these numbers.

$\frac{1}{4}$ of 24 = ☐ $\frac{1}{3}$ of 18 = ☐

$\frac{1}{2}$ of 50 = ☐ $\frac{1}{10}$ of 70 = ☐

$\frac{1}{5}$ of 40 = ☐

6. Write the answers to these addition and subtraction questions.

36 + 29 = ☐	65 – 39 = ☐
45 + 41 = ☐	238 + 9 = ☐
93 – 81 = ☐	527 – 11 = ☐

7. Read each question. Write the answer.

540. Count on 4 tens. _____

630. Count back 4 tens. _____

320. Count on 4 hundreds. _____

545. Count back 3 hundreds. _____

8. Write the answers to these questions.

How many days are there in one week? _____

How many months are there in a year? _____

How many days are there in a leap year? _____

🔲 **End-of-year assessment**

Name _____ Date _____

9. Write the answers to these word problems.

Jon bought five bars of chocolate at 30p each.

How much change did he get from £2? _____

Sam bought 30 stickers. She already had 59 stickers.

Then she gave her brother 40 stickers.

How many stickers does she now have? _____

The tape needs to be cut into five-metre lengths. There are 48 metres

on the roll. How many five-metre lengths can be cut? _____

How much tape is left over? _____

10. Mark the right angles in these shapes.

11. Draw the lines of symmetry in these shapes. One shape does
not have any lines of symmetry. Put a cross beside it.

12. Sort the numbers 50 to 100 onto this Venn diagram.

Numbers 50 to 100

Multiples of 5

Class record sheet

Names

Key objectives: Year 3												
Read, write and order whole numbers to at least 1000; know what each digit represents.												
Count on or back in tens or hundreds from any two- or three-digit number.												
Recognise unit fractions such as 1/2, 1/3, 1/4, 1/5, 1/10, and use them to find fractions of shapes and numbers.												
Know by heart all addition and subtraction facts for each number to 20.												
Add and subtract mentally a 'near multiple of 10' to or from a two-digit number.												
Know by heart facts for the 2, 5 and 10 multiplication tables.												
Understand division and recognise that division is the inverse of multiplication.												
Use units of time and know the relationships between them (second, minute, hour, day, week, month, year).												
Understand and use £.p notation.												
Choose and use appropriate operations (including multiplication and division) to solve word problems, explaining methods and reasoning.												
Identify right angles.												
Identify lines of symmetry in simple shapes and recognise shapes with no lines of symmetry.												
Solve a given problem by organising and interpreting numerical data in simple lists, tables and graphs.												

Answer sheet

ASSESSMENT

Autumn term

Week 7
P87 **Money** Answers will vary.
P89 **Right angles** Answers will vary.
P90 **Money and word problems** 1) 130p, £1.30; 270p, £2.70; 575p, £5.75; 645p, £6.45. 2) £3, £2; £4.75, 25p; £2.70.
P91 **Assessment test: autumn half-term 1**
1) Forty five; Ninety eight; One hundred; One hundred and thirty four; Two hundred and nine; Five hundred and sixty. 2) 63; 89; 106; 348; 909; 990. 3) 300, 50, 1; 600, 0, 2; 900, 50, 0; 500, 10, 7.
4)

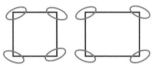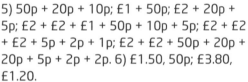

5) 50p + 20p + 10p; £1 + 50p; £2 + 20p + 5p; £2 + £2 + £1 + 50p + 10p + 5p; £2 + £2 + £2 + 5p + 2p + 1p; £2 + £2 + 50p + 20p + 20p + 5p + 2p + 2p. 6) £1.50, 50p; £3.80, £1.20.

Week 14
P95 **Guess the number** Answers will vary.
P97 **Fraction count** 12, 8, 6; No; No; 24 cannot be divided exactly by 5 or 10; 10, 5, 4, 2; No; 20 cannot be divided exactly by 3.
P98 **Fractions, word problems and Carroll diagrams** 1) 1/2; 1/4; 1/3; 1/5; 1/10. 2) 40; 11; 20. 3) Multiples of 5: 20, 25, 30, 35, 40, 45, 50; Not multiples of 5: 21, 22, 23, 24, 26, 27, 28, 29, 31, 32, 33, 34, 36, 37, 38, 39, 41, 42, 43, 44, 46, 47, 48, 49. Answers to the second part will vary.
P99 **Assessment test: autumn half-term 2**
1) 65, 75, 85, 95; 216, 206, 196, 186; 443, 543, 643, 743; 707, 607, 507, 407. 2) 7; 365 (366 in a leap year); 52; 12. 3) 1/4; 1/10; 1/5; 1/3. 4) Answers will vary. 5) Ready salted; 33; chilli; 4; lamb and mint sauce and smoky bacon; Probably not; Different number of children in the class, different likes and dislikes.

Spring term

Week 7
P103 Cover it No answers.
P105 School time 94; 7; 60; 7.
P106 At the park 2½ hours; £6.50; 12 metres; 91.
P107 Assessment test: spring half-term 1
1) 10; 30; 100; 40; 18; 35; 30; 14; 60; 14; 60; 20. 2) 2; 8; 5; 4; 5; 9; 5; 2; 8; 9. 3) 5 x 4 = 20; 4 x 5 = 20; 10 x 2 = 20; 2 x 10 = 20. 4) 30; 15; £3 or 300p; £5.25.

Week 13
P111 Division hop 5; 5; 10; 6; 8; 5; 7; yes; 6; 6; 7; 9; 8; 6; 7; yes; no; 6; 9; 4.
P113 Favourite fruits Answers will vary.
P114 Number sort Numbers inside circle: 50, 52, 54, 56, 58, 60, 62, 64, 68, 70, 72, 74, 76, 78, 80, 82, 84, 86, 88, 90, 92, 94, 96, 98, 100; Numbers outside circle: 51, 53, 55, 57, 59, 61, 63, 65, 67, 69, 71, 73, 75, 77, 79, 81, 83, 85, 87, 89, 91, 93, 95, 97, 99.
P115 Assessment test: spring half-term 2
1) 8, 8 ÷ 2 = 4 or 8 ÷ 4 = 2; 25, 25 ÷ 5 = 5; 60, 60 ÷ 10 = 6 or 60 ÷ 6 = 10; 18, 18 ÷ 2 = 9 or 18 ÷ 9 = 2; 100, 100 ÷ 10 = 10; 35, 35 ÷ 5 = 7 or 35 ÷ 7 = 5; 18, 18 ÷ 3 = 6 or 18 ÷ 6 = 3; 27, 27 ÷ 3 = 9 or 27 ÷ 9 = 3; 12, 12 ÷ 3 = 4 or 12 ÷ 4 = 3; 20, 20 ÷ 2 =10 or 20 ÷ 10 = 2. 2) 8; 20; 12; 9. 3) Numbers inside circle: 3, 6, 9, 12, 15, 18, 21, 24, 27, 30; Numbers outside circle: 1, 2, 4, 5, 7, 8, 10, 11, 13, 14, 16, 17, 19, 20, 22, 23, 25, 26, 28, 29.

Answer sheet

Summer term

Week 7
P119 Make a number No answers.

P121 Alphabet search No lines of symmetry: F, G, J, L, N, P, Q, R, S, Z; 1 line of symmetry: A, B, C, D, E, K, M, T, U, V, W, Y; 2 lines of symmetry: H, I, O, X.

P122 Challenges 1) 63, 86, 264, 573, 24, 49. 2) 8. 3)

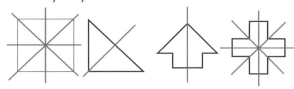

P123 Assessment test: summer half-term 1
1) 132, 156, 199, 305, 350, 402, 405, 406, 436, 461, 465, 466, 497, 555, 654, 679, 695, 697, 769, 796, 799, 967, 976, 999. 2) 525; 493; 912; 445; 71; 85; 66; 24; 93; 26; 92; 19. 3) 74; 41. 4) No answers.

Week 14
P127 Beat the clock No answers.

P129 Make a total Answers will vary.

P130 Venn and Carroll diagrams Answers will vary.

P131 Assessment test: summer half-term 2
1) 19; 3; 15; 7; 20; 18; 9; 0; 9; 8; 7; 12; 7; 23; 14; 15; 4; 19; 1; 16. 2) ✓; ×, 37; ×, 83; ✓; ×, 76; ×, 54; ×, 24; ✓; ×, 85; ×, 88. 3)

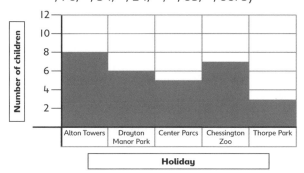

End-of-year assessment

P134 Mental maths test 1 1) 943; 2) 3; 3) 106; 4) 17; 5) 9; 6) 5; 7) 16; 8) 30; 9) 70; 10) 8; 11) 14; 12) £2.10; 13) 86;
14)

15) irregular pentagon; 16) 5.

P136 Mental maths test 2 1) Four hundred and six; 2) 8; 3) 489; 4) 8; 5) 14; 6) 19; 7) 50; 8) 8; 9) 80; 10) 3; 11) 35 minutes; 12) £4.00 or 400p; 13) 3;
14)

15)

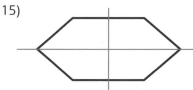

16) 21.

P138 Check-ups 1) 17; 20; 8; 9; 7; 19; 8; 0; 4; 5; 14; 45; 100; 12; 35; 80; 40; 18; 40; 2. 2) 5; 4; 3; 4; 7; 32. 3) 535; 607; 440; 329. 4) 100, 10, 9; 300, 20, 0; 400, 0, 8; 600, 90, 9. 5) 6; 25; 8; 6; 7. 6) 65; 86; 12; 26; 247; 516. 7) 580; 590; 720; 245. 8) 7; 12; 366. 9) 50p; 49; 9; 3 metres.
10)

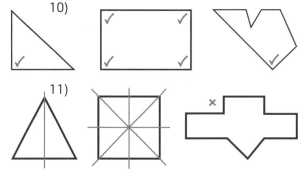

11)

12) Numbers inside circle: 50, 55, 60, 65, 70, 75, 80, 85, 90, 95, 100; Numbers outside circle: 51, 52, 53, 54, 56, 57, 58, 59, 61, 62, 63, 64, 66, 67, 68, 69, 71, 72, 73, 74, 76, 77, 78, 79, 81, 82, 83, 84, 86, 87, 88, 89, 91, 92, 93, 94, 96, 97, 98, 99.

In this series:

ISBN 0-439-96512-8
ISBN 978-0439-96512-5

ISBN 0-439-96513-6
ISBN 978-0439-96513-2

ISBN 0-439-96514-4
ISBN 978-0439-96514-9

ISBN 0-439-965152
ISBN 978-0439-96515-6

ISBN 0-439-965160
ISBN 978-0439-96516-3

ISBN 0-439-965179
ISBN 978-0439-96517-0

ISBN 0-439-965187
ISBN 978-0439-96518-7

To find out more, call: 0845 603 9091
or visit our website www.scholastic.co.uk